SCENES FROM THE PAST: 16 (PART

THE MIDLAND ROUTE FROM M

PART TWO

CHEADLE HEATH TO CHINLEY

Chinley Station, late 1930s: Class 2 4-4-0 No.**323** belonging to 19D (Heaton Mersey) awaits departure from platform 5 with a Down stopping train. Taken on what was clearly a beautiful day, the strong side lighting gives a sharp emphasis to the standard Midland Railway-pattern nameboards and gas lamps. *Collection of R.G.Chapman*

E. M. JOHNSON

Copyright © Foxline Publishing and E. M. Johnson.
ISBN 1 870119 21 5
All rights reserved
Designed and Edited by Gregory K. Fox.
Typeset by Bill Rear, Johnstown, Wrexham.
Printed by The Amadeus Press, Huddersfield.

Published by Foxline Publishing,
32 Urwick Road, Romiley, Stockport. SK6 3JS

Acknowledgements

A full acknowledgement was made in volume I to my valued contributors. Via their good offices , they have, again, allowed me access to their valuable material for this work. For this I am ever grateful and I would like to thank all of them for their unstinting genorosity; without their help this book would not have been possible. Mention this time must be made of Alan Barnard, whose archives covering Gowhole Yard have enlivened a sorely-neglected spot. Brian Green delved through train registers and shunting records and his own notes to answer all manner of queries. From the Chinley area came valuable help from Norman Birkett, a former Station Inspector there, and Frank Coupland who provided some very interesting pictures.
Re-tracing our steps towards Manchester, Bill Wood loaned some extremely interesting pictures taken in the area of the Throstle Nest Junctions. This is a very important contribution; not only was the area a veritable thicket of lines and junctions, it had been seldom photographed and I must express a special "thank you" to Bill for his diligence. Others who have helped by way of providing pictures and much useful material are:

David Birch
Sam Cowan
Malcolm Cross
Kenneth Field
Martin Graty
Brian Hilton
Basil Jeuda
Norman Jones
The Museum of Science & Industry in Manchester
E.R.Morten
Eric Oldham
Wallace Sutherland
Mrs. Carol Swainston
Douglas Thompson
Melvin Thorley
Martin Welch

from Cheadle Heath ....

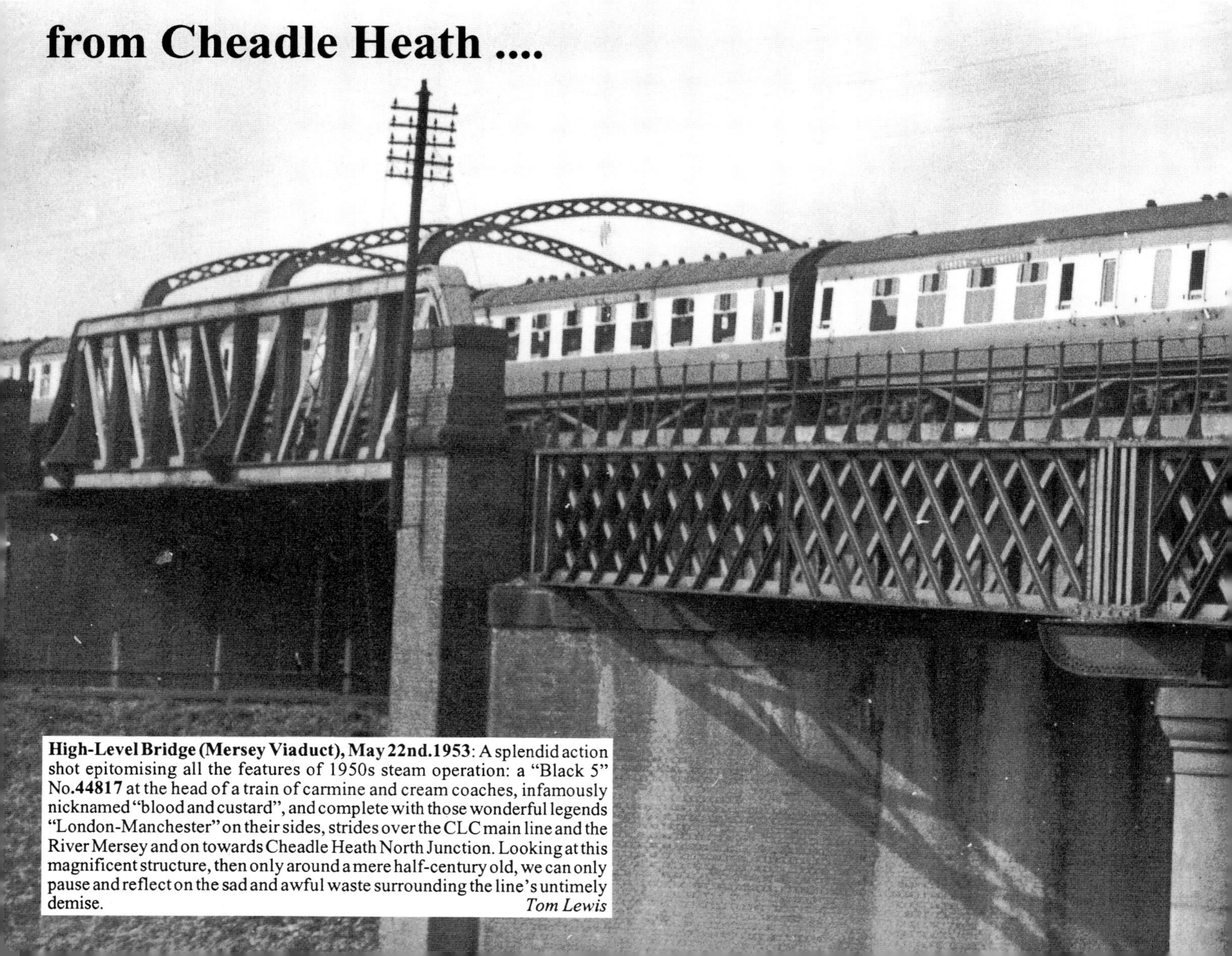

High-Level Bridge (Mersey Viaduct), May 22nd.1953: A splendid action shot epitomising all the features of 1950s steam operation: a "Black 5" No.**44817** at the head of a train of carmine and cream coaches, infamously nicknamed "blood and custard", and complete with those wonderful legends "London-Manchester" on their sides, strides over the CLC main line and the River Mersey and on towards Cheadle Heath North Junction. Looking at this magnificent structure, then only around a mere half-century old, we can only pause and reflect on the sad and awful waste surrounding the line's untimely demise. *Tom Lewis*

Foreword

As mentioned in the previous book in this two-part work, this volume takes a look at the "new" line-the New Mills and Heaton Mersey Railway, opened fully on July 1st.1902 between Heaton Mersey Station Junction and New Mills South Junction. The story also encompasses the remainder of the "old" route-the Midland line of 1867-from New Mills itself up to Chinley.

If the enthusiasm of youth is detected in this work, then, perhaps, that is appropriate, and in some ways ironic. Appropriate because I got to know the"new" line as a teenager in the 1950s. In those heady days, when many of the Manchester-bound expresses stopped at Chinley, we liked nothing more than to return home on one of them to Manchester Central. Finding an end vestibule near to the engine, it was heads out all the way as the train cavorted along the 19 or so mile downgrade; through Disley Tunnel, where the window had to come up!, over the viaduct at Hazel Grove, then on to Cheadle Heath and through Didsbury and Withington like a hurricane. For, make no mistake about it, this was a fast line. Cecil.J.Allen, the doyen of train recorders, timed "Britannia" No.**70014** *Iron Duke* at 89 m.p.h. between Cheadle Heath and Didsbury in 1959 and there are unofficial, though authentic, accounts of trains passing through Didsbury at close on 100 m.p.h.

And there is irony too. Irony because this Midland line was the last of the links in a North/South "London" chain designed to combat and fight off the mighty LNWR. Yet, like the Great Central, it has been severed-though not as drastically-and the LNWR have had the last laugh. "Last in, first out" seems to have afflicted much of our railway system, as closure and rationalisation have become the order of the day. Though the "new" line still exists, albeit minus any stations and bereft of any services through to the south, its primary function has long been withered away.

Yet, we can still watch trains on at least one section of this grandly-designed route. Still, the Hoppers run and even steam has returned to Chinley North Junction on occasions since 1968. Sad, though, that we can no longer travel south via Peak Forest and Millers Dale to Derby and then St.Pancras. Somebody once said that amongst the first passengers on a time machine there was sure to be a railway enthusiast. Until that supreme piece of science fiction appears, it is only via our memories and books like this that we can re-live the past. Your seat is reserved, I wish you a pleasant journey.

E.M.Johnson.
Burnage, Manchester. July, 1992.

..... to Chinley

Chinley Station, north end May 17th.1952: From behind the North Junction signalbox we are provided with a splendid view of the area at the top of the station. The goods yard is alongside, the 5-ton crane in front of the timber goods shed ready for action. In modern times Messrs. Bernard Wardle, textile finishers, were the biggest users of freight and parcels facilities at Chinley: 3 "Vanfits" being needed every day for the dispatch of their traffic. The door to the goods warehouse was later demolished during a shunting accident. Taking centre stage is Derby-based LMS Compound No.**40927** looking quite smart in its lined black livery complete with early "British Railways" insignia; its 4-coach train will almost certainly be a Derby-Manchester "stopper." Pulling away from platform 6, it is travelling on what was known as the "Down Outside" road, effectively a loop line off the Down Fast. To the right of this can be seen the "Straight Road" and next to this, running through the goods shed, the "Warehouse Road." *B.K.B.Green*

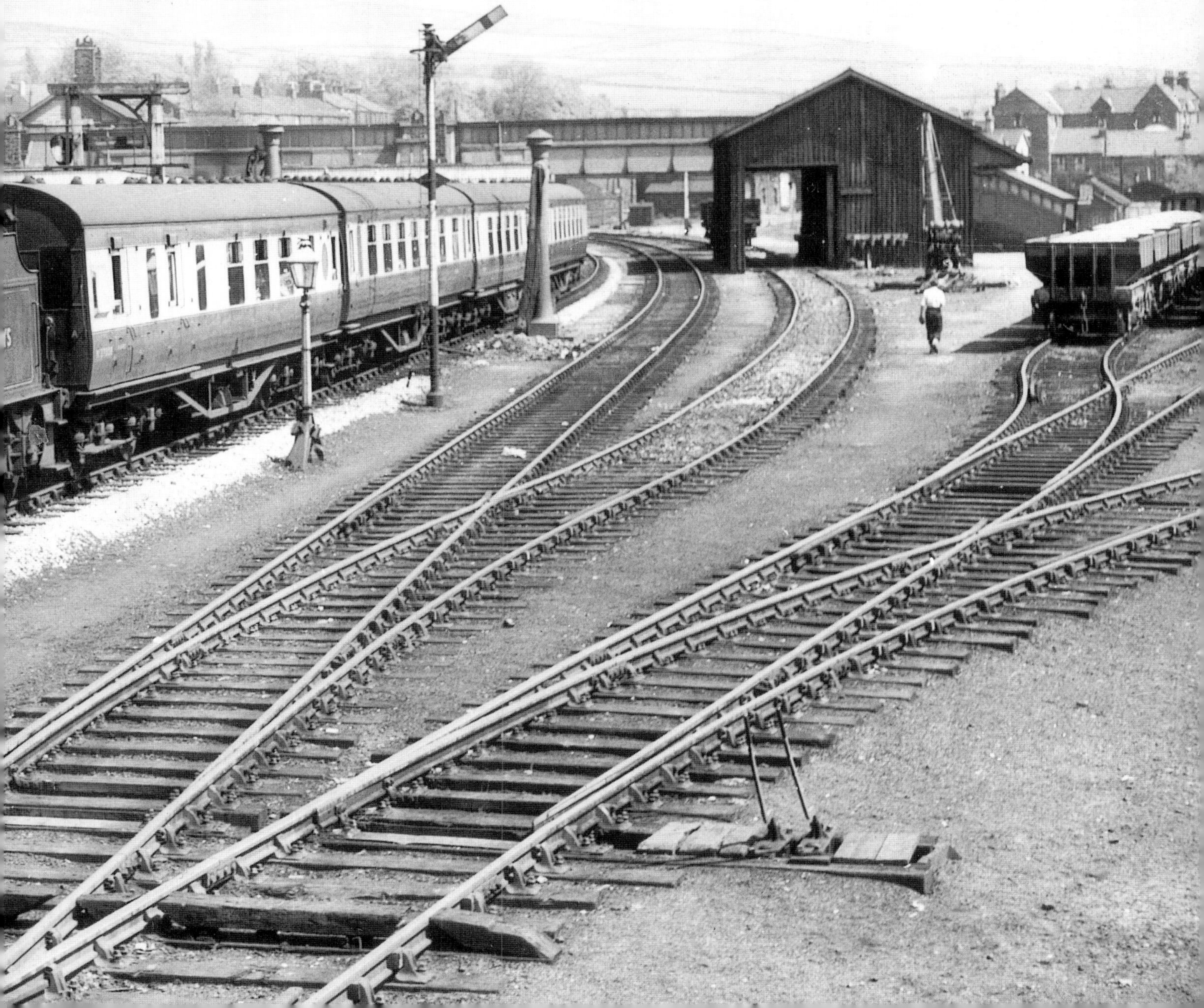

Contents ...

DEDICATION

I would like to dedicate this book to my mother, Muriel Johnson, a most kindly and gentle soul, whose shopping trips to Didsbury always included time for "Ted" to watch the trains at that splendid little station.

Heaton Mersey Station Junction, May 31st.1952: This most striking portrayal of a "Jubilee" in action comes from the camera of the late Tom Lewis, a photographer whose pictures have a drama and impact that is the prerogative of just a few cameramen. No.**45628** *Somaliland* is caught passing over the Vale Road underbridge, just south of Heaton Mersey Station, and storming along towards the Mersey Viaduct and Cheadle Heath with a London express. Behind is Heaton Mersey Station Junction box, the Down Home and slotted Distant for Didsbury standing in front. *Tom Lewis*

Cheadle Heath North Junction, June 26th.1952: "Jubilee" No.**45694** *Bellerophon* storms past Cheadle Heath North Junction box on a beautiful summer afternoon with an Up express. The fireman is busy with the exhaust steam injector and a white feather lifts from the safety valves in readiness for the arduous 17-mile climb beginning here and continuing all the way up to Peak Forest. Those of us who watched express trains in steam days will remember the anticipation felt as we stood on the end of a platform. Maybe, as at Cheadle Heath, we were within the sound of a signalbox and could hear the block bell announcing the train's passage at a distant location. Levers would crash over, signal wires squeaked and semaphore arms swung skywards. A few minutes later a black shape would appear on the horizon, growing gradually larger and accompanied by a thunderous roar which rose in volume, crescendo-like, ever and ever louder. We would turn and watch, always in awe, as the "Jubilee", "Scot", "Britannia", Class 5 or whatever, disappeared down the line, motion whirring and carriage bogies rattling over the rail joints, to enthral yet one more time.

As we will see in this second volume, Cheadle Heath was an important staging post in the Midland's last thrust towards Manchester. The scene at North Junction shows the layout very clearly. In the left of the picture the so-called "Liverpool Line" curves away down to Cheadle Junction to join the CLC line. This ran through Northenden, Skelton Junction, Partington and Cadishead to connect at Glazebrook East Junction with the same concern's line from Manchester Central to Liverpool. Protecting the crossover from the Derby to the Liverpool lines is a fine Midland-pattern bracket semaphore controlled from the equally splendid period III signalbox. Through the summer haze in the background can be seen the high-level bridge that carried the 1902 line high over the River Mersey and the CLC line from Tiviot Dale.

B.K.B.Green

Cheadle Heath

Few railway companies possessed such all-conquering ambitions as did the Midland. Determination to penetrate territory belonging to rivals seemed to permeate the company's thinking. What other company, indeed, would have contemplated building such a line as the Settle and Carlisle - driven against all odds through some of the most hostile terrain in the British Isles? Cheadle Heath came about as part of such thinking. Constrained by congestion and slow progress around Marple and Stockport, the Midland were to have one final thrust at completing a direct line through to Manchester. The result was the New Mills and Heaton Mersey Railway which had been authorised by an Act dated August 6th.1897. This cut-off line ran from New Mills South Junction through Disley Tunnel, Hazel Grove, Bramhall Moor Lane and Cheadle Heath to Heaton Mersey. The boring of the 3,800 yard Disley Tunnel alone was an expensive proposition. The total cost of the new nine and three-quarter mile railway cost the company £2M. The section from New Mills, including the Disley Tunnel, was built by Messrs.Walter Scott and Co.; the northern section from Hazel Grove down to Heaton Mersey was constructed by Messrs.H.Lovatt. This part was opened first-from Heaton Mersey to Cheadle Heath-on October 1st.1901 and was used by stopping passenger trains to and from Manchester Central. The second portion of the line, and this included the "Liverpool Curve" round from Cheadle Heath North Junction to Cheadle Junction on the CLC, was first used by goods trains on May 4th. 1902 and by passenger trains on July 1st. that year. Cheadle Heath was conceived on a grand scale with ample facilities. Both goods and carriage sidings were provided, together with a spacious goods warehouse, along with a 60 ft.turntable and ample watering facilities. Platform accommodation consisted of two islands and one single platform. The southern-most platform was a bay, while the two northern faces served the Liverpool line which split from the Derby-Manchester line at Cheadle Heath South Junction. Turning away from the Manchester line at Cheadle Heath North Junction, the Liverpool line joined up with the CLC Godley to Glazebrook line at Cheadle Junction.

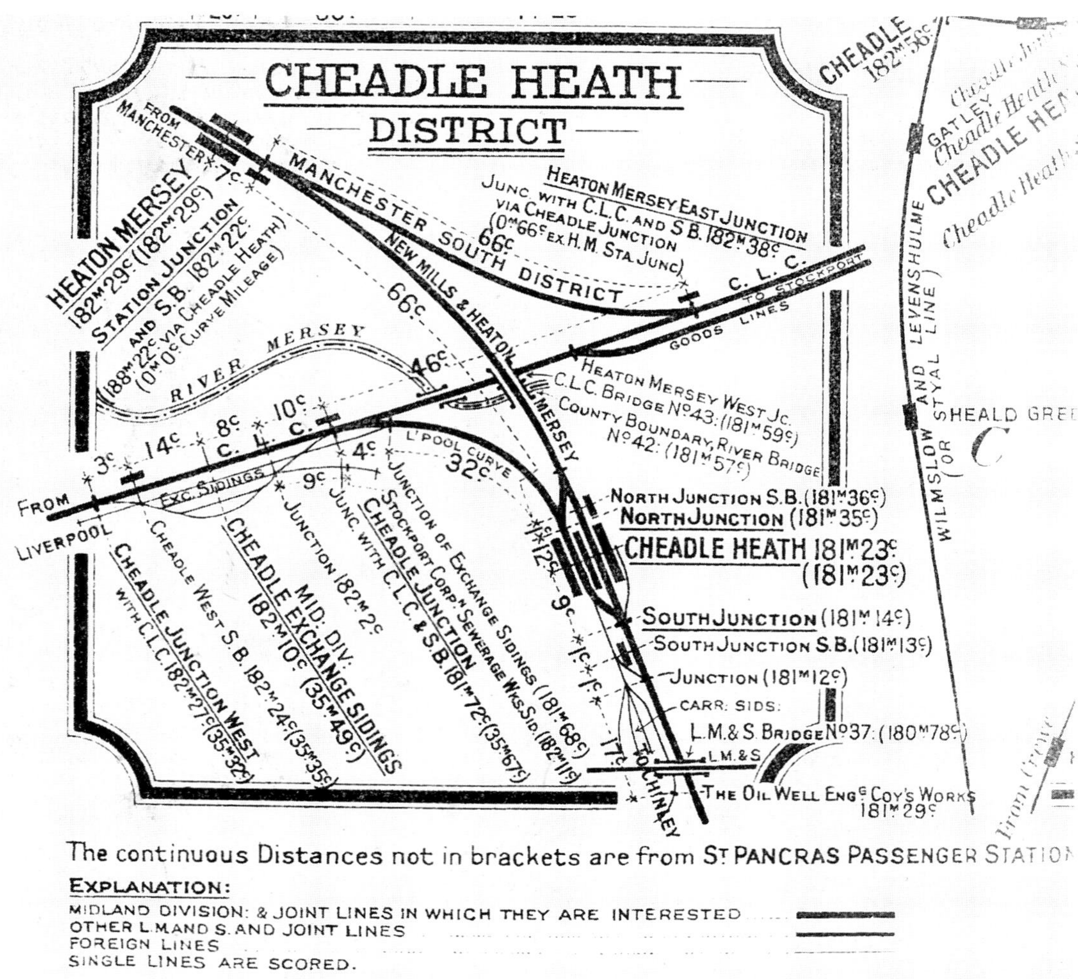

Cheadle Heath North Junction, May 16th.1959: From behind the signalbox at Cheadle Heath North, "Britannia" Pacific No.**70021** *Morning Star* approaches with the 7.25 morning express to St.Pancras. This picture gives a good illustration of the layout at the north end of the station: the sweeping crossovers allowing traffic to cross to and from the Liverpool and Manchester line; the Liverpool line itself can be seen curving away on the right to join the CLC down at Cheadle Junction. 8F 2-8-0 No.**48017** waits at the Up Liverpool line home signal with the returning "Hopper" empties en route back to Tunstead Quarry for another load of limestone. Once the Pacific has cleared the station the "Hoppers" will run through the Liverpool line platforms and join the Derby line at Cheadle Heath South Junction. *Raymond Keeley*

Cheadle Heath North Junction, July 26th.1952: Hughes/Fowler 0-8-0 No.**49552** comes cautiously off the Liverpool line with an Up train of wagon empties. The Cheadle Heath South Junction Distant is "on"-no doubt the train is to be held pending the passage of an Up express on the Derby line. Though the bulk of railway pictures have tended to depict passenger trains hauled by prestigious engines, it is good to see a shot such as this, depicting an everyday humdrum freight working. Freight was the lifeblood of the railway, and of the country's industry and therefore its economy. Sad, indeed, that so much of it has been sacrificed to that great god, Road. *B.K.B.Green*

Cheadle Heath North Junction, September 18th.1965: With exhaust steam injector on, Class 5 No.**45057**, a Speke Junction engine, comes off the Liverpool line at Cheadle Heath North with a train of seventeen "Presflo" cement wagons bound, almost certainly, for Earles Sidings at Hope, Derbyshire. Though modern upper-quadrant signals are in evidence the Midland influence is still apparent here, manifested by the splendid signalbox and the starting signal on the Down Liverpool line. The two photographers probably viewed our Class 5 with some disdain. Almost certainly they were waiting for the LCGB's "High Peak Rail Tour" hauled from Waterloo as far as this point by No.4472 *Flying Scotsman*. From Cheadle Heath, local celebrity Jubilee No.45705 *Seahorse* was booked to take over. "Seahorse" was a regular performer on the 5.22 Manchester Central Buxton "Club Train" at that time. *Author's collection*

Cheadle Heath. early 1960's. From the window of the carriage on an Up express, this view shows the approaches to Cheadle Heath station from the Manchester direction. The bridge carrying Stockport Road frames the Derby line to the left with those serving Liverpool trains and local stopping services, to the right. *M.S. Cross.*

Cheadle Heath station, August 3rd. 1957: Here the photographer is standing on the east side of Edgeley Road, the thoroughfare that runs off the A560 Stockport to Altrincham road towards Shaw Heath and the A6. Dominating the background is the impressive-looking goods shed and offices, behind this the seven goods sidings fanning out towards Stockport Road. Standing at the Up Liverpool line platform is Class 5 No.**44842** with a 9-coach Rhyl to Sheffield excursion. This train will have travelled along the CLC line via Skelton Junction, Northenden and Cheadle before turning off at Cheadle Junction to call here. Running through the centre of the picture are the Up and Down lines to and from Heaton Mersey Station Junction. *J.W.Sutherland*

Cheadle Heath n.d: The summer of 1958 saw the arrival for the first time ever of Pacifics performing regular duties on Manchester Central-St.Pancras expresses. Even in those comparatively recent times information about engine and train workings never filtered through as quickly as it does today. I still remember the sensation felt at seeing 70015 *Apollo* hurtling through Didsbury on a Down afternoon express. Awakening happy memories of those far-off days is this splendid shot by Tom Lewis of No.**70031** *Byron* storming through the Manchester platforms with an Up express. Just visible under the footbridge are the Liverpool lines curving away to the left and their attendant pointwork at Cheadle Heath North Junction.
Tom Lewis

Cheadle Heath station n.d: From alongside the goods yard we take an opposing view to that seen previously. On this fine summer day Johnson 0-6-0 No.**2991** is busily engaged with part of the daily toil of yesteryear's rail scene-that of moving the single wagonloads of merchandise in a bustling freight yard. Though other company's goods vehicles,inevitably, appear in the picture the scene here is the quintessence of Midland practice. The elegant little Johnson engine, complete with tender cab, was the first of a long series of 0-6-0 tender designs; 2991 was built by Neilsons in 1876 and some lasted right up until 1964. Elsewhere, the company's hallmark is evident: platform canopies, resembling those at Morecambe, gas lamp standards, signals, station furniture, fencing, and the well-known station name, or running-in boards.
Author's collection

CHEADLE HEATH

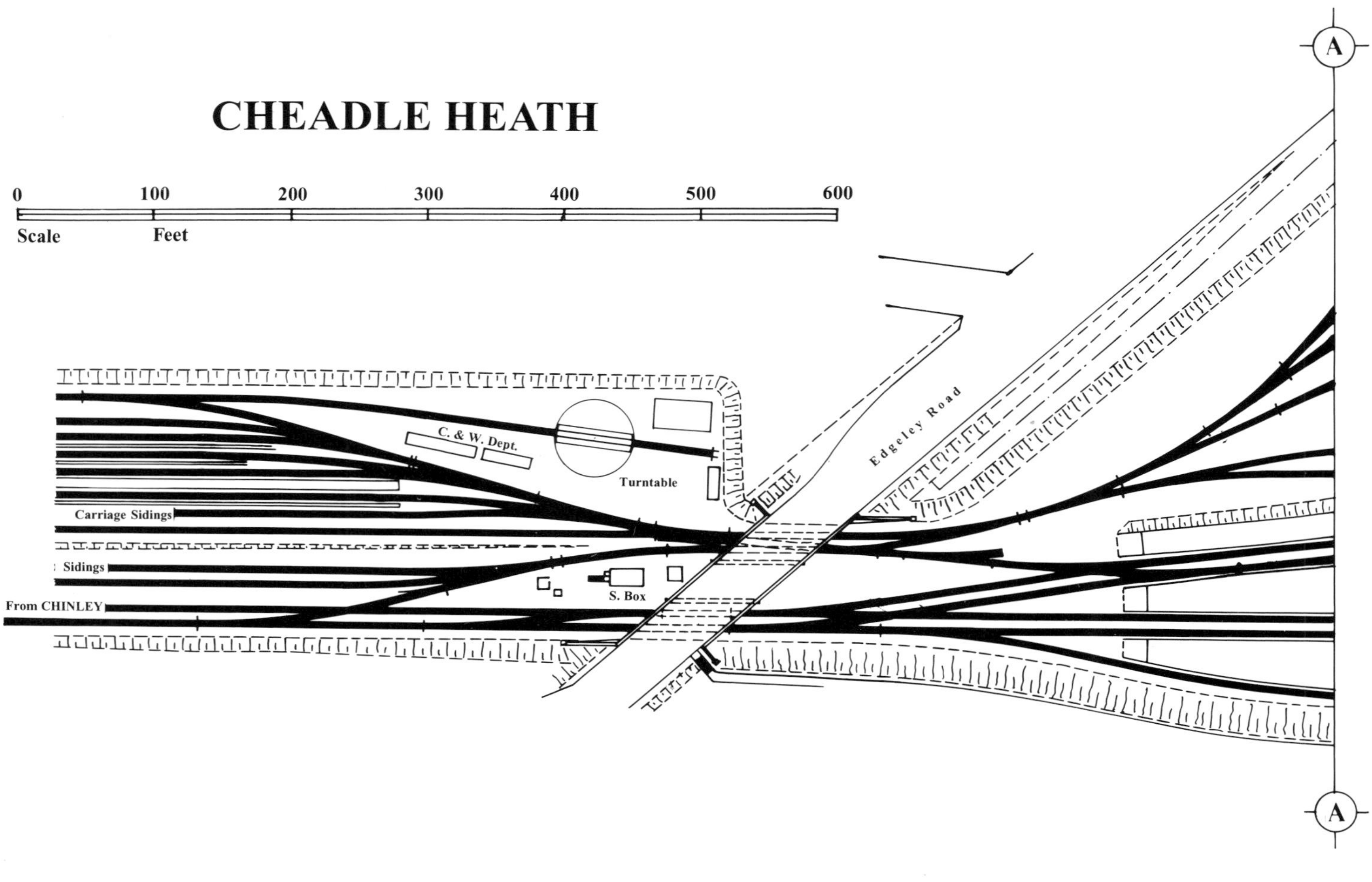

Cheadle Heath, carriage sidings, n.d: A scene with the human touch. The stalwart performers of the South District local services in pre-Grouping days, as we have seen, were the Deeley 0-6-4 tanks. At the south end of the carriage sidings, just by Edgeley Road, No.**2008**, pauses obligingly for the photographer. The character stood to the right of the picture is a guard and makes an interesting comparison with his counterpart in the picture of the 2-4-0 at Withington in volume I. No.**2008** is coupled to a Bain arc-roofed bogie carriage, examples of which we have already seen. The stock was still gas-lit at this stage, a practice the Midland company was to be heavily criticised for in the wake of the two catastrophic accidents on the Settle and Carlisle line before the First War. *E.Pouteau*

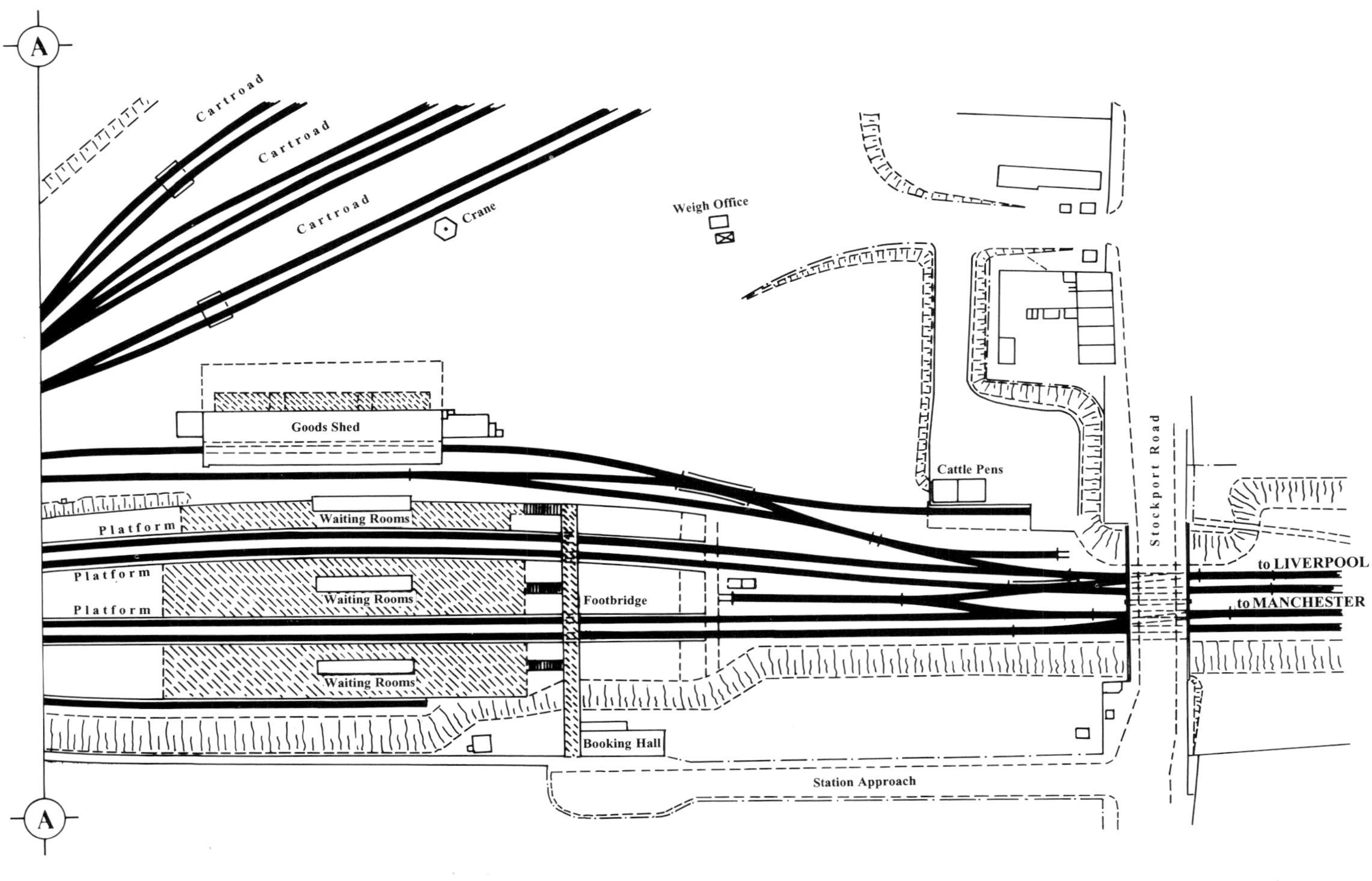

Cheadle Heath c.1922: Deeley "Flatiron" 0-6-4 tank No.**2004** awaits departure at the Down Manchester platform with a stopping train for Manchester Central. Entrance to Cheadle Heath station was gained via a footpath from Stockport Road; this was situated behind the boarded fence visible above the front of the locomotive. The building in the background housed (left to right) the Stationmaster's office, booking and parcels office and booking hall. Once past the booking hall passengers passed straight onto the footbridge which connected with the three platforms.
Railway Revivals collection

Cheadle Heath (sidings by goods warehouse) n.d: In front of the goods shed ran a long siding from which it was posssible to reach either the cattle pens, a shunting neck, or the Liverpool line. This vintage view shows rebuilt Johnson 4-4-0 No.**331** paused in front of the warehouse with an afternoon Cheadle Heath to Liverpool train. It will be awaiting the arrival of the St.Pancras-Liverpool through carriages from a Down Manchester express. The coach behind the tender is a Midland Clayton 12-wheeled lavatory brake composite built in 1896 to Diagram 522. These coaches all entered LMS stock and were withdrawn between 1928 and 1936.
Railway Revivals collection

Cheadle Heath, April 14th.1966: Waiting at the Up Manchester Platform is the celebrated "Midland Pullman" (7.45 ex Manchester Central) paying its usual early morning call here en route for St.Pancras. Sadly, this was the Pullman's penultimate trip through Cheadle Heath before being replaced, the following week, by the new, electrically-hauled, Pullman service from Manchester Piccadilly to Euston. Hereafter, the Midland line would begin the final part of its downward spiral which resulted in eventual closure in 1969. Cheadle Heath had a special place in the history of this celebrated Pullman train. When proving trials were taking place in 1960 between Derby and Cheadle Heath, the 6-car beauty would run as far as the Starter on the Down Liverpool line before reversing and completing its run back to Derby. On Monday, July 2nd.1962, a local resident, Mr.Charles Minifie, of Cheadle, had the distinction of being the 100,000th. passenger to travel on the Pullman. Mr.Minifie was given VIP status for the day; he was accompanied by a management delegation from Manchester and was given the privilege of a cab-ride as far as Cheadle Heath. An engraved ash tray completed his special trip and an anniversary cake was prepared for the train crew. We complete this glimpse of Cheadle Heath by looking over to the Liverpool line platform where Class 25 No.**D5279**, in two-tone green livery, waits for the road with a train of returning ICI Hopper empties for Tunstead Quarry. *A.C.Gilbert*

Cheadle Heath South Junction, n.d: Following hard on the heels of the "Britannia" debut on the St.pancras expresses were the celebrated "Peak" Diesels. Using a 1-Co-Co-1 wheel arrangement and weighing in at at 133 tons, these Type "4" machines eventually became the much-loved Class 40 and 45 locomotives of more recent times. From this somewhat sharper angle at the south end of Cheadle Heath station **D76** is seen pulling away with a 9-coach train. Cheadle Heath was a useful pick-up and set-down point for passengers in this part of Stockport and its environs, several trains making the call there including the celebrated "Midland Pullman." Concrete lamp standards and maroon enamelled signs are now the order of the day, the goods yard is fairly busy, and indeed, the whole place still looks reasonably prosperous. *Tom Lewis*

Cheadle Heath South Junction, May 10th.1948: A quiet moment at Cheadle Heath. Perhaps the stillness of early summer on Edgeley Road, behind the photographer, is interrupted on the odd occasion by the passage of a number 74 bus or, maybe, the clatter of horses' hooves- yes, this was still quite a common mode of transport in those days! The doll at the end of the goods yard has been raised to allow 3F No.**3533**, engaged on the daily "pilot", to draw ahead under the bridge towards the carriage sidings. On prominent view is the sweeping trackwork, uncluttered by trains and revealing the formation from the Derby line to the Liverpool line over by the warehouse. *J.D.Darby*

Cheadle Heath, goods yard 1920s: A grimy Johnson 3F tank, No.**1951**, vigorously propels an interesting assortment of coal wagons during part of its daily duty as yard "pilot." A touch of local flavour is added by the sight of a wagon belonging to Linney Brothers Ltd. of Heaton Mersey. Permanent Way materials are in abundance in the foreground although there is no official evidence to suggest such a depot here. *Railway Revivals collection*

Cheadle Heath, (turntable and water tower) early 1920s: Cheadle Heath's locomotive facilities were on the opposite side of Edgeley Road, facing the top of the carriage sidings that were laid out parallel to the running lines. On the 60 foot turntable an unidentified 8F 2-8-0 is being turned; the table had no vacuum assistance, notice the crew in a forward-moving position giving an "all-out" effort; the railway company did provide a slatted timber staging around the table to give a secure foothold! To the left of the turntable is one of the redundant Midland coach bodies that did duty here for so long. Shown on the LMS rating plan as "stores", in later years it was supplemented by the body of a former Pullman vehicle which was used as mess accommodation-prestigious facilities indeed! *Collection of M. Thorley*

Cheadle Heath South Junction, May 10th.1948: Standing back somewhat from the viewpoint of the first picture we come to the Edgeley Road overbridge to look at ex-LNW G2A or "Super D" 0-8-0 No.**9136** coming off the Liverpool line to join the Derby line with a train of empty wagons which seems to stretch for ever into the distance. At Cheadle Heath South the Liverpool and Manchester lines parted company, movements controlled by the signalbox which stood between Edgeley Road and the adjacent carriage sidings. Closer study of the picture reveals a station little changed from Midland days; save, perhaps for the two-armed "doll" controlling exit from the yard. My Summer 1957 ABC "Combined" tells me that No.**49136**, as this engine became, had been withdrawn by then. *J.D.Darby*

Cheadle Heath South Junction, July 28th.1951: Nine empty hopper wagons and a brake van are behind the tender as 8F 2-8-0 No.**48340** slogs away up towards Adswood and Bramhall Moor lane. To the left can be caught a glimpse of the carriage sidings; between the LMS 57 ft. suburban coach and the loco, a peep at the Midland Pullman body mentioned in the previous text can just be gleaned. Through the loco's exhaust we can see the junction home signal pulled off for the Down Liverpool line platform. South Junction signalbox stood in front of the Edgeley Road bridge and is just visible behind the first hopper wagon. *B.K.B.Green*

Cheadle Heath South Junction c.1952: A visitor from the "foreign" camp, in the shape of ex-LNER J10 0-6-0 No.**65160**, pauses in the course of the daily shunt in the goods yard-sited between the Down main line and Edgeley Road. The Cheadle Heath North Junction Down Liverpool line Distant issues a caution to a loaded ICI limestone train wending its way past en route to Northwich.
Collection of Eric Barnard

Cheadle Heath South Junction n.d: From almost the same spot as the adjacent picture, we look at a returning "Hoppers". From 8F 2-8-0s in steam days, these ICI Hopper trains have had an interesting variety of Diesel power over the last twenty-two years or so. In perfect summer lighting Type 2 (later Class 24) No.**D5277**, in two-tone green livery, brings a 14-plus train of Hopper empties off the Liverpool line and heads south once more towards the Peak and Tunstead Quarry. *Tom Lewis*

Cheadle Heath, 1949: Our last picture at Cheadle Heath takes us to the south of the station. Standing on what was known as "Edgeley Footbridge"-the footbridge that spanned the running lines and the carriage sidings, we take a look south. Coming up to Cheadle Heath South Junction is Midland 4F No.**44022** at the head of a 24-wagon coal train. In the background, a freight train makes its way over the LNWR's Edgeley Junction to Northenden line. Silhouetted against the sky, the wagons and their spoked wheels have taken on an almost Lowry-like appearance, such is the effect of the light. The LNWR line had opened as far back as 1866; bridge No.37 was built in 1900 and consists of two spans, each 26 ft.wide. The span on the right crossed the private siding that ran off to serve the Oil Well Engineering Company's works. *Author's collection*

South of Cheadle Heath, n.d: Cheadle Heath and the LNWR's line from Edgeley Junction are left behind as LMS Compound No.**41060** pulls away with a 4-coach stopping train. To the right of the picture can be observed the sidings and "parachute" water column at Cheadle Village Junction. *Tom Lewis*

South of Cheadle Heath, June 12th.1950: Impressive the steam locomotive was, environmentally-friendly it often was not! 4F No.**44573** is having a spot of firing trouble, its black pall of smoke darkening the sunny summer sky. The train has just cleared the attractively-named Lark Mill footbridge and is making its way towards the district of Adswood. To the left of the picture, behind the footbridge, is the works of what was then the Oil Well Engineering Company on Bird Hall Lane.
Tom Lewis

Adswood Sidings, April 26th.1958: "Jubilee" No.**45627** *Sierra Leone* is making good progress up the 1-in-100 towards Bramhall Moor Lane. A clean, sharp exhaust is at the chimney, the exhaust steam injector is on and the middle cylinder drain cock is open; nothing to stop her now! The train is a 9-coach Liverpool to Derby express. Trains from the Midlands cities to Liverpool ran into Manchester Central before reversing out again, although there are instances on record of some services using the Throstle Nest curve in order to run directly to the Lancashire port.
Tom Lewis

Adswood Sidings, April 11th 1952: Caprotti Class 5 No.**44757** storms past Adswood sidings with a 9-coach Manchester Central to St.Pancras express. This and the previous picture were taken from the overbridge carrying the LNWR Manchester-Crewe line over the railway here. Off to the right are the extensive sidings that paralleled the LNWR line on the Down side and were built on land called "Daisy Field." Today, the sidings are long gone, and the Midland line exists only as a single track carrying sparse traffic. Adswood and Lark Mill footbridges can be seen in the background. *B.K.B.Green*

Jackson's Sidings: Stanier 2-6-2 tank No.**40132** with the daily morning "trip" working from Heaton Mersey. The loco pulls energetically out of the yard, notice the brake van parked on the Down line. *Collection of M.Thorley*

South of Adswood, March 22nd.1952: No selection of photographs showing freight trains along this stretch of railway could be complete without a look at one of the ICI Hopper trains. Here is 8F No.**48527** clearing the LNWR line overbridge taking its load of empties back to Tunstead Quarry for yet another load of broken limestone. In the right background is the overbridge carrying Adswood Road over the railway. To the rear of the train was the site of the siding serving the brickworks of Messrs.J & A.Jackson. *B.K.B.Green*

Past milepost 181 the ascending gradient eased to 1-in-140. Under Garner's Bridge (No.29) and the railway lighted upon the location known as Bramhall Moor Lane. A 20-lever signalbox here controlled the Up and Down lines as well as a 15 chain lay-by siding on the Up side. A single-road goods shed and siding were opened on July 1st.1902, the day the line opened for passenger traffic. In later years, two sidings were provided on the north side of the line for Messrs.Mirrlees, Bickerton, & Day Ltd. (now Mirrlees). The goods depot closed on January 30th.1965 and the signalbox on November 12th.1967. No passenger facilities were ever provided here.

Bramhall Moor Lane, May 18th.1952: The Hawthorn blossom is in full flower to frame this wide-angle shot of "Jubilee" No.**45650** *Blake* at the head of a Down express. Clearing Bramhall Moor Lane, steam is shut off as the driver makes the most of the down grade all the way now until just before Manchester Central. It is noticable that the formation and structures along this stretch of line are sufficient to accommodate another pair of tracks. *B.K.B.Green*

Bramhall Moor Lane, 1946: A slight steam leak does not seem to be perturbing the fireman of "Jubilee" No.**5649** *Hawkins* as it charges along the up grade towards Bramhall Moor Lane with an 11-coach express. The locomotive, though somewhat grimy, appears to be wearing the short-lived black, lined maroon and straw livery with block numerals applied as the new post-War LMS standard from 1946. *P.Ward*

Bramhall Moor Lane, 1946: Bramhall Lane and Garner's Bridge are left behind as an unidentified J39 blackens the sky up the 1-in-140 at 9.30 p.m. with the 8.22 Deansgate to Colwick goods train. Mention was made of these workings in the Chorlton-cum-Hardy feature; they continued over this line until 1952 before closure of the spur line from Brinsley to Codnor Park forced their diversion on to the Woodhead route. Pictures of single wagonload express freight trains are rare enough in this period; the Deansgate to Colwick rarer still because of the time of day it ran. A special bouquet, therefore, to Peter Ward for providing this exceptional shot. *P. Ward*

Bramhall Moor Lane, n.d: From trackside views we raise our sights a little to look down the line towards Adswood and Cheadle Heath with Bramhall Moor Lane in the background; Messrs.Mirrlees' works are standing off to the right. En route back to the pits of Yorkshire, Derbyshire and Nottinghamshire are the 30-odd empty wooden-bodied coal wagons seen in this splendid study by the late Tom Lewis. Hauled by "Austerity" 2-8-0 No.**90267**, the train will soon clear the sylvan surroundings of south-east Stockport and enter the sepulchral gloom of Disley Tunnel. *Tom Lewis*

Clear of Bramhall Moor Lane, the line continued to rise steadily at 1-in-110 towards milepost 178. Beyond here there was a short respite at 1-in-120, easing to 1-in-200 at Hazel Grove station. Hazel Grove station seems to have suffered from a classic case of poor siting. It was situated on the east side of the Norbury Viaduct that spans the Macclesfield and Buxton roads and was approached via a long footpath from the direction of High Lane. Not surprisingly, traffic receipts were sparse: just 1,486 passengers were booked through between July 1st. and December 31st.1902. As a consequence, train services were reduced in 1903 to give only 5 Up and 3 Down trains calling there each day. Little improvement took place over the years 1903-1916; a high spot for receipts appears to have occured in 1916 when just £237 was taken! Not surprisingly, Hazel Grove closed for business on January 1st.1917. Perhaps if the station had been sited nearer to the village, on Chester Road, it might have fared better. Such a situation, though, would have made it a near neighbour of the LNWR's Hazel Grove station and it is doubtful, anyway, that the Midland station would have survived the rigours of later rationalisation plans.

Between Bramhall Moor Lane and Hazel Grove, n,d: Several footbridges over the"new" line were characterised by their lattice steelwork as we have already seen. Another such example is Hatherlow Lane, spanning the tracks in the background here. That dominant motive power force of the 1950s, the ex-LMS "Jubilees", are to the fore again as No.**45628** *Somaliland*-with an 8-coach Up express-pours forth a plentiful exhaust contrasting with the billowing, fleecy Spring cloudscape. *Tom Lewis*

Between Bramhall Moor Lane and Hazel Grove, n.d: LMS Compound No.**41173** sullies the atmosphere as it passes over the Chester Road bridge, between Hazel Grove and Poynton, with a Manchester to Sheffield stopping train. With Hatherlow lane bridge in the background, we recall to mind a scheme of 1931 at this point to connect the LNWR Stockport to Buxton line, running on the skew under here, with the Midland line by means of a short connecting line. Thus was first hatched a plan put into operation by BR in 1986: the Hazel Grove Chord. *Tom Lewis*

Hazel Grove, April 7th. 1951: Bramhall Moor Lane's Down Distant is "off" and the site of Hazel Grove station is left behind as LMS Compound No.**40929** crosses Chester Road underbridge and runs rapidly down the 1-in-200 with a Grand National excursion working-a Nottingham to Aintree special. At Cheadle Heath South Junction the train will be signalled to take the Liverpool line from where it will run over the CLC via Northenden and Skelton junctions down to Glazebrook East Junction. Joining the CLC Manchester to Liverpool line here, 40929 and its train will head towards Halewood Junction from where it will proceed north-westwards onto the Southport line through the suburbs of a great city: Gateacre, Childwall, Knotty Ash and West Derby to Aintree itself-home of the world's greatest steeplechase. Just for the record, *Nickel Coin* won the day. *Tom Lewis*

Hazel Grove Station, n.d: Few pictures survive to show the Midland Railway's station at Hazel Grove. This little nugget, taken from a contemporary postcard, looks along the line in the Up direction, towards Disley Tunnel. Two lie-by sidings were provided here on the Down line and housed 43 wagons; on the Up side, beyond the island platform, was a single siding with a set-back from a point just beyond the signalbox, this siding housed 52 wagons. The Down sidings were taken out of use on November 12th. 1972. Gazing on this scene, as if from another world now, we can admire the simple architectural lines of the wooden canopy and attendant buildings, also of wood, on the single island platform. The tiered arrangement of the canopies is unusual, set this way, doubtless, to match the gradient profile. A Belpaire-boilered 4-4-0 is seen on the left-hand side of the picture, whilst a station official-possibly the station master or a senior ticket collector-stares along the line. Trips to Cardiff and Newport were on offer when this picture was taken, but the fares and details are not discernible. The far end of the platform carries one of the Midland company's distinctive angled running-in boards; bearing the station's name in 12" letters, it is just visible between the end of the canopy and the signalbox. *B.Jeuda collection*

Hazel Grove Station, August 26th.1960: The station buildings have long gone and only the grass-grown island platform remains as a reminder of this short-lived quasi-rural station. 4F No.**44023** rumbles past with the 9.25 Cheadle to Gowhole freight comprising, mostly, wooden-bodied coal wagons. Just visible at the back of the train is the edge of the Norbury Viaduct. Open woodland gives an indication of the relative remoteness of the site, a situation still extant today. *Gordon Coltas*

Hazel Grove. c.1965. Sited at the end of the island platform, this was Hazel Grove's signal box, a standard Midland Railway period III design exhibiting windows extended all round almost to floor level. As is clearly seen here, the structure was situated between the running lines, the train, from which the picture was taken, being on the Up line, heading towards Disley tunnel. The station platforms, the ramp of which can be just seen in the left hand corner, were reached via a subway (Bridge No.18) - on the Down side - at the Cheadle end. *M.S. Cross.*

Hazel Grove c.1946: Class 5 No.**4817** storms past the site of Hazel Grove station with an Up express, the outline of the signalbox can just be made out in the background. The station consisted of a single island platform and, though closed in 1917, the buildings remained in situ for many years. *P.Ward*

Between Hazel Grove and Disley Tunnel, n.d: This lovely, pastoral view shows us "Jubilee" No.**45614** *Leeward Islands* clearing the Hatherlow Lane (Bridge No.25) footbridge heading towards Hazel Grove; Rutter's Lane is in the background. The train is W496-the Summer Saturdays only 11.40 a.m. from Colwyn Bay to Sheffield Midland and recalls with special affection the happy holidays spent by Mancunians, and many of us in the North of England, on the North Wales coast. *K.Field*

Between Hazel Grove and Disley Tunnel, March 1st.1951: Almost at the same spot, this crisp, winter view exemplifies the wasteful operation of double-heading which had been endemic in locomotive practice on Midland routes since time immemorial. With only four corridor coaches and a van between them, Class 5 No.**44815**, and an unidentified LMS Compound, are making a great deal of effort with what is a mere bagatelle for a load. *J.D.Darby*

Five large-scale works had been necessary in building the "new" line from New Mills South Junction to Heaton Mersey. These were: Newtown Viaduct-240 yards long and spanning land and the River Goyt west of New Mills South Junction, Disley Tunnel-2 miles, 346 yards long-and three years in the making, Norbury Viaduct spanning the Buxton and Macclesfield roads near to Hazel Grove station, Cheadle Heath station-with its two junctions and complex of facilities and the Mersey Viaduct-135 yards long-that carried the line over the Mersey and the CLC line between Cheadle Heath and Heaton Mersey. Of these works, the Disley Tunnel was the grandest and the most expensive.

Approaching Disley Tunnel, September 29th.1951: The magnificent three-arched brick-built structure known as Threaphurst Lane (bridge No.12) frames this view of Compound No.**41181** engaged on a Manchester Central to Derby train. Disley Tunnel is now just about 175 yards away, just time for the driver and fireman to take evasive action! Notice the typical Midland features in the design of the bridge, notably the brick "roll" separating the arch ring from the spandrel wall. The letter "C" on the warning notice on the left-hand side indicated commencement of a temporary speed restriction. *Tom Lewis*

Disley Tunnel, West Portal, n.d: This was the view seen by engine crews as their charges plunged into the suffocating two and a quarter mile gloom of Disley Tunnel on a steadily rising 1-in-132 gradient. Running over the top of the tunnel is the Great Central and North Staffs. Joint line from Marple Wharf Junction along to Macclesfield Central; High Lane Station is a quarter of a mile off to the right. Not visible on the reproduction is the wording on the stone tablet over the tunnel mouth: M.R.DISLEY TUNNEL 1901. A wooden notice board in the cutting on the right gives the length as 3866 yards. *D.Ibbotson*

Disley Tunnel, East Portal, n.d: Out of the gloom and into the sunlight comes No.**45694** *Bellerophon* (son of Glaucus, King of Corinth) with his Up express bound for St.Pancras (Roman Martyr). Their stint through the tunnel finished, the crew have a short respite on level ground before the line begins to climb in earnest: rising to a maximum of 1-in-90 with the rigours of the fiendish 1 mile, 56 chain Dove Holes Tunnel, between Chapel-en-le-Frith and Peak Forest, still to conquer. *Tom Lewis*

Disley Tunnel, East Portal, n.d: The familiar Midland Railway Wyvern is set off above the tunnel mouth. Comparisons with the east portal are interesting: notice the facing work here is done entirely in stone, not brick and to a totally different design. The year of completion and the owning company are, again, set off: this time in two stone tablets inlaid either side of the portal. Notice the catch point designed to prevent errant vehicles running away along the down grade into the tunnel. *D.Ibbotson*

Disley Tunnel, East End, n.d: As well as being famous for its beautiful scenery, the Peak District is notorious for the appalling weather which often prevails in winter. Emerging from Disley Tunnel with an Up express is "Royal Scot" No.**46140** *The King's Royal Rifle Corps* storming through conditions straight off the proverbial Christmas card and making for a spectacular photographic display. In reality, the conditions are not too onerous and, doubtless, hardened railwaymen in the Derbyshire area would dismiss this snow blanket as a mere trifle. *A.H.Bryant*

A. H. Bryant: A Profile

This book and its predecessor are made all the richer by the inclusion of many photographs taken by the late Alan Bryant. Through the good offices of his widow, Mrs.Winifred Bryant, and his close friend, Maurice Daniels, I have been able to put together this short profile; I offer it as a tribute to a man who was, without a doubt, one of the North West's leading railway photographers.

Alan Howard Bryant was born in Hazel Grove in 1927. The railway bug seems to have bitten him early on in life and he began his photographic expeditions with his mother's box camera before he left school. Alan learned his railway "trade" at Adswood Sidings on the Stockport to Crewe line in the 1930s. His notes record that he would often cycle down to this busy spot as early as 7.45 in the morning to observe the proceedings. One of his most vivid memories was the sight in Crewe Works of "Coronation" Pacific No.**6235** *City of Birmingham* resplendent in red and gold livery in the summer of 1939.

Alan had married in 1948. The family lived, appropriately enough, at number 6, Railway Terrace, Disley just overlooking the Buxton line and from where Alan was able to aim his camera to good effect at the nearby lineside. A memorable picture was that of the preserved LMS Jubilee "Bahamas" engaged on shunting duties in Disley goods yard! Daughter Barbara often accompanied him on his numerous railway forays, and his keen love and affection for his subject rubbed off, too, on his wife, Winnie.

Though he served an apprenticeship at Fairey Aviation as an aircraft fitter, life on the railway seemed to hold greater appeal and he began work as a shunter at Longsight in 1948. Alan moved to Davenport Station as a Leading Porter and then to Middlewood Lower on the Stockport to Buxton line in the same post. The world of manufacturing beckoned him back around 1955, however, when he began work at an engineering company in Whaley Bridge, then as a "reelerman" at J.Makin's paper mill. Makin's mill, now the home of the Disley Paper Company, was sited by the southern portal of Disley Tunnel and the company had their own siding, accessed from the Down line. It was at and around this location that Alan took some of his finest action shots. My own two favourites are reproduced in this book and both depict "Scots" in action; one shows No.**46116** *Irish Guardsman* caught in a swirl of action with the Down "Palatine" as it roars past a returning ICI Hopper empties. The other classic reveals the bare winter landscape around Disley as No.**46140** *The King's Royal Rifle Corps* plods along through the winter snows with an Up express.

Alan Bryant had that rare knack in railway photography of being able to keep his subject as complementary to the surrounding

Disley from Waterside Footbridge, looking East: The wild, open look of the Peak landscape is seen to good effect as this unusual view of a returning Hopper empties unfolds before us. Scoured by the passage of thousands of tons of bulk limestone, the insides of the wagons present a white, almost pristine appearance, this in contrast to the brownish exterior, sullied by years of running up and down these tracks and now, without a doubt, B.R.'s oldest rolling stock. *Tom Lewis*

landscape; the subject matter is never allowed to predominate or intrude, yet in those same scenes, the train is not subservient either. He was an avid big format man-using a Pentacon 6 for the bulk of his work, along with some photographs taken on glass plates. A couple of trusty Pentaxes were retained for his colour slides. As with many people who treat their work as an art-form, Alan was a member of the Royal Photographic Society and achieved the high echelons of that organisation by becoming a Fellow. Nearer to home, Alan was a member of the Manchester Amateur Photographic Society (MAPS).

Neither did his talents just extend to photographic coverage of the full-size railway scene. He was also a keen railway modeller, being an active member of both the Macclesfield and Hazel Grove societies. Alan wrote articles, mostly prototypically-based, for Railway Modeller and was also a contributor to Railway World, Railway Magazine and Trains Illustrated.

Alan Bryant's photographic work extended to churches, aircraft and birds, and though these are subjects outside of a work such as this, to look upon the range and scope of his activities is to realise that here, indeed, was a man of many talents. Alan died suddenly in 1989; his work is a fitting testimony to those abilities, long may we admire them.

* * * * * * * *

Disley Tunnel, East End, April 1963: Leaving Disley tunnel on the Up line is a 9F 2-10-0, number unknown, with a lengthy freight made up almost entirely of empty 16-ton BR standard mineral wagons. The ubiquitous steel-bodied vehicles make an interesting comparison to the earlier pictures of freights on this line with their content of wooden-bodied wagon stock. Spanning the tracks here is another lattice girder bridge. This is bridge No.9 which rejoiced in the name of Waterside Footpath; it provided a viewpoint for many of the fine pictures taken here. *Tom Lewis*

Set immediately to the east side of the tunnel mouth were two sidings, one on either side of the line; each siding had a short neck at either end. The Down siding, existing originally only as a lie-by, was made in to a goods loop in June 1955. It was also equipped with a short siding which served the paper mill belonging to J&J.Makin Ltd. Access to Makin's siding was controlled by a single-lever ground frame. Controlling operations at the east end of Disley Tunnel was a small signalbox; named plain "Disley", it had opened with the line in May, 1902 and later acquired a new lever frame. It closed on June 9th.1968. Both the goods loop and the sidings have since been removed.

Disley Tunnel,East End, n.d: An Eastern Region engine for a change: B1 4-6-0 No.**61008** *Kudu* sails blithely along in beautifully fine and clear summer conditions with a yet another trainload of empty coal wagons. In the early part of 1957, *Kudu* was allocated to Leicester (G.C.) shed. *A.H.Bryant*

Disley Tunnel, East End, n.d: Taken from the other side of the Waterside Footpath, we look towards the tunnel mouth to watch that star of the early 1960s, the *Midland Pullman* making its Up journey. By the looks of the spreading foliage, the Up siding does not handle much traffic! Milepost 174 sits opposite the signalbox. *A.H.Bryant*

Disley from Waterside Footbridge, looking East, n.d: Just one wagon lingers at the end of Makin's Paper Mill siding as a 4F (a "Derby 4" to the local railwaymen) No.**44172**, coupled to a self-weighing tender, from 17C (Coalville) runs past and heads towards the tunnel with a Down mixed freight. *A.H.Bryant*

Disley from Waterside Footbridge, looking East, n.d: The amazing diversity of freight traffic handled by the railways, even in comparatively recent times, is exemplified as we watch 8F No.**48005** drift towards Disley Tunnel with a trainload of agricultural tractors. No less than around forty such vehicles are being conveyed, each securely anchored to a short-wheelbase flat wagon. A commonplace at the time, such a train would cause something of a sensation nowadays! *A.H.Bryant*

Disley from Waterside Footbridge, looking East, n.d: A chance moment with a camera can often present a fascinating shot, though opportunities giving a result like this are few and far between. All the noise, rush and atmosphere of steam railway operation areseen here as "Royal Scot" No.**46116** *Irish Guardsman*, in charge of the Down "Palatine" (7.55 a.m. ex St.Pancras, 11.45 into Manchester Central), passes a returning Hopper empties clattering past at speed, almost certainly with an 8F in charge. The running of the Limestone Hopper trains has been big business since Hopper-type wagons, each capable of carrying up to 44 1/2 tons of limestone, were introduced in 1936. Tunstead Quarry is now the biggest limestone working in Europe with an annual output exceeding some 5 million tons.

A.H.Bryant

Disley from Waterside Footbridge, looking East, July 1960: A strong feature of steam day operation was the amazing variety of trains that would turn up, especially on a summer Saturday such as this. Dusty corners of sheds were scoured and almost any loco capable of turning a wheel would be pressed into service. The 9F 2-10-0s had acquitted themselves very well indeed; as passenger engines they had proved capable of running at speeds in excess of 80 m.p.h! This unidentified specimen has steam in hand as it passes the Down goods loop and drifts towards the tunnel entrance with a 10-coach excursion train-reporting number M78.

Tom Lewis

Red House Lane Bridge, n.d: Two more trains for the price of one! "Jubilee" No.**45652** *Hawke* makes rapid progress and a rather smokey exit from Disley Tunnel with an Up Manchester Central-St.Pancras express. Caught by the camera, another express thunders over Red House Lane bridge (No.8) and hurtles towards the confines of the tunnel. *A.H.Bryant*

East of Disley Tunnel, May 3rd.1952: Compound No.**41173** makes good progress with an Up 6-coach express along one of the few level stretches of the line. Quickly, the gradient will rise again-at 1-in-100/1-in-90 before New Mills South Junction is reached. Notice the Down Home signal exists as a single entity, the adjoining bracket and "doll" for the Down Goods Loop (still over three years off) have yet to be added. *B.K.B.Green*

Between Disley and New Mills South Junction, n.d: "Britannia" Pacific No.**70042** *Lord Roberts*, one of the six Pacific transfers to the Midland line in 1958, roars over Burymewick Road bridge and on towards New Mills South with an express. The "Britannias" put a new lease of life into the Manchester-St.Pancras expresses during their brief tenure. Their coming, however, was not without incident. One engine, No.**70014** *Iron Duke*, broke its drawbar near Bramhall Moor Lane on a Down express. Thankfully, the design of the locomotive, with its extended footplate between cab and tender, saved the crew from a fatality. *A.H.Bryant*

Between Disley and New Mills South Junction, n.d: Its smokebox sillhouetted against the backdrop of hills, "Jubilee" No.**45579** *Punjab* rounds the bend in the line under Marshall's bridge, making for a dramatic effect as it storms along to New Mills South Junction with an Up express. *A.H.Bryant*

Between Disley and New Mills South Junction, n.d: Approaching Marshall's bridge, on the Down line, is "Royal Scot" No.**46142** *The York and Lancaster Regiment* with an express from St.Pancras. Just to the east of this location, about three-quarters of a mile from New Mills South Junction itself, was the delightfully-named location of Knat Hole Wood. A signalbox existed at Knat Hole and had been opened with the line, on May 4th. 1902. The box was closed, as an experiment, in January 1905 and was never re-opened. It was demolished in July 1909. *A.H.Bryant*

New Mills, c.1955: The railway's practice of referring to short tunnels as "covered ways" was referred to in the Marple feature in the previous volume. Here is another such example: bridge No.3 was known in the Midland's Bridge Register as "Albion Road Covered Way." Here it is, a 90 yard-long structure, stone faced and complete with retaining wall. In the background, further up the line, is the Woodside Road overbridge; names such as this are now impinging on the railway, indicating that the countryside is receding and the townscape encroaching once again. Milepost 173 completes the picture. *D.Ibbotson*

Newtown Viaduct, n.d: One of the less glamorous aspects of railway work was the examination of bridges, more often than not carried out under dirty and wet conditions and, frequently, in the hours of darkness. Larger structures could not easily be visually examined from close quarters and, in the case of multi-span bridges and retaining walls, it became necessary to call upon the services of the rail-mounted viaduct inspection unit. Popularly known as "The Gozunda", this hydraulically-operated unit, mounted on a former LMS Bogie Bolster wagon, was self-propelled, but at such low speeds (20 ft./min.) as to make the facility unattractive. Latterly, alternative power was sought in the shape of a 400 h.p. Diesel Shunter whose low gearing was ideal for the "walking pace" movement required. **D3770** provides the motive power, and a Sunday possession of the line between New Mills South Junction and Cheadle Heath is in force, as engineers carry out an inspection of bridge No. 1- Newtown Viaduct. Leo Kelly and an assistant are perched high above the River Goyt in the cradle of their unit. The train is on the Up line, facing south towards Chinley. Modellers should take note of the "roll" in the stonework, mentioned elsewhere, and the design and siting of the Midland Company's cast-iron bridge plate.

Newtown Viaduct, same day: A broader view showing the Viaduct Inspection Unit at work, no doubt the feeling on the platform was exhilarating! At least one instance, on the Western Region, is recorded of the failure of the hydraulic system on a "Gozunda"-the unfortunate occupants having to spend a night in freezing temperatures before a rescue could be mounted. Such are the perils of railway work. One "Gozunda" of this type is preserved on the Llangollen Railway and was used in the restoration of the Dee Bridge, just to the west of the town. *Both photos-Martin Welch*

Newtown Viaduct, n.d: Crossing over the line and facing west, towards New Mills South Junction, we see a loaded Hopper train clearing the thirteen arches, each one is visible!, and rolling down the 1-in-90 away from the junction. To the left of the track is the splitting Distant signal for New Mills South Junction: right for the Fast line, left for the Goods, or Slow line. The 16 loaded Hopper wagons present a formidable load: the train seen here has a gross weight of around 1100 tons. Each wagon weighs some 22 tons tare and carries either 43½ or 44½ tons of stone (depending on the type of bogie). In steam days, 17 loaded Hoppers was the maximum for a Class 8 engine. In January 1957 a 9F 2-10-0 was tested on these trains and No.**92045** handled 19 wagons, reportedly without any difficulty. In recent times, the maximum load I have recorded on these trains was 22 loaded wagons-seen at Navigation Road on July 13th.1987 hauled by a Class 47 Diesel. *A.H.Bryant*

Newtown Viaduct, n.d: 16 chains west of New Mills South Junction is Newtown Viaduct which carries the "new" line over land and the River Goyt. The viaduct, 245 yards long, consists of thirteen arches, 45ft. wide, two of which span the river, the remainder the land on either side. Standing on the east side, nearest to New Mills South Junction, we watch 8F No.**48135** charging up to the junction with a train of limestone Hopper empties; "14 on" plus the brake van. Notice the stone "roll"-mentioned previously-between the arch ring and the spandrel wall giving the structure a typical Midland look. On view also, is the "standard" Midland wooden post and rail fencing. *P.Ward*

New Mills South Junction, June 16th.1951: Thirty years or so on from our last picture takes us into the early years of British Railways with 4F No. **44185** slogging past the junction and up the 1-in-90 towards Gowhole and Buxworth. Around 36 empty wooden-bodied coal wagons are behind the tender. Our Midland Railway bracket signal controlling the "old" line has given way to an LMS-pattern tubular post variety; notice the revised semaphore arrangement from pre-war days. In the foreground is the signalbox, this dated from the opening of the Disley line and housed 55 levers. Curving away towards Disley the "new" line crosses the River Goyt via Newtown Viaduct; some of the thirteen arches can be glimpsed in the corner of this magnificent view. *B.K.B. Green*

New Mills South Junction

New Mills South Junction was the focal point of the Midland's last thrust into Manchester; for it was from here, north to Heaton Mersey via Disley Tunnel and Cheadle Heath that the "new" or "cut-off" line opened in 1902. Coupled with this was the quadrupling of the railway south via Bugsworth to a much enlarged station at Chinley. (Enabled by the Chinley and New Mills Widening Act of 1900). What had been a quiet Derbyshire village had, all of a sudden, a measure of greatness thrust upon it. These days, when pretty well all expansion of the nation's transport system is connected with new motorway construction, it is difficult to comprehend the nature and scale of these, some of the last great works of the Midland company: the construction of nine and three-quarter miles of brand-new double track railway with the 3,800 yard Disley tunnel, not to mention the associated embankments and viaducts; the widening of some three miles of line to quadruple track through Bugsworth to Chinley and on to North Junction (including the removal of Bugsworth Tunnel); the freight concentration yard at Gowhole-opened in 1903. The provision of an entirely new and enlarged station complex at Chinley completed this impressive list.

New Mills South Junction 1930s: An introduction to this fascinating location is provided by the sight of rebuilt Class 2 4-4-0 No.**485** coming up the "new" line from Disley Tunnel. Off to the right of the train is the "old" line via Romiley whose tracks formed the Down and Up Slow lines from this point to Buxworth Junction. Here we are well into LMS days-witness the use now of standard-pattern Stanier coaching stock and the replacement of the "new" line bracket signal by one of upper-quadrant pattern. This uses corrugated steel arms first tried out by the LMS in the mid 1920s; though of Midland pattern, the bracket itself is new and carries the standard flat cap, LNWR-style, on top of the posts. Notice that all the spectacle casings are now painted white, another LMS innovation.

E.R.Morten

New Mills South Junction c.1920: Here we look from Marsh Lane, the thoroughfare that parallels the line here, across the junction itself. Waiting at the Home signal at the end of the Up goods line before crossing onto the Up Slow line (originally the "old" line) is a Deeley "Flatiron" with, for a change, a freight working. Behind the engine can be seen the sweeping crossings taking traffic to and from the "old" and "new" lines. Thus could trains be switched at New Mills South from one set of lines to the other and vice-versa. The New Mills and Heaton Mersey line officially commenced at a point mid-way between the two sets of crossings. A myriad of telegraph wires give a sure indication of the volume of traffic once handled here. Below the Home signal is the fixed Distant for Gowhole Goods Junction.

Sam Cowan

New Mills South Junction, August 6th.1949: In complete contrast to the previous pictures at this location we move to more modern times as Class 5 No.**45385**, still with "LMS" on the tender, pulls an 11-coach Blackpool to Sheffield excursion away from the junction. The exhaust steam injector is busily topping up the boiler ready for the long slog up to Chinley and beyond before the west end of Cowburn tunnel is reached and the gradient eases downhill towards Sheffield. *J.D.Darby*

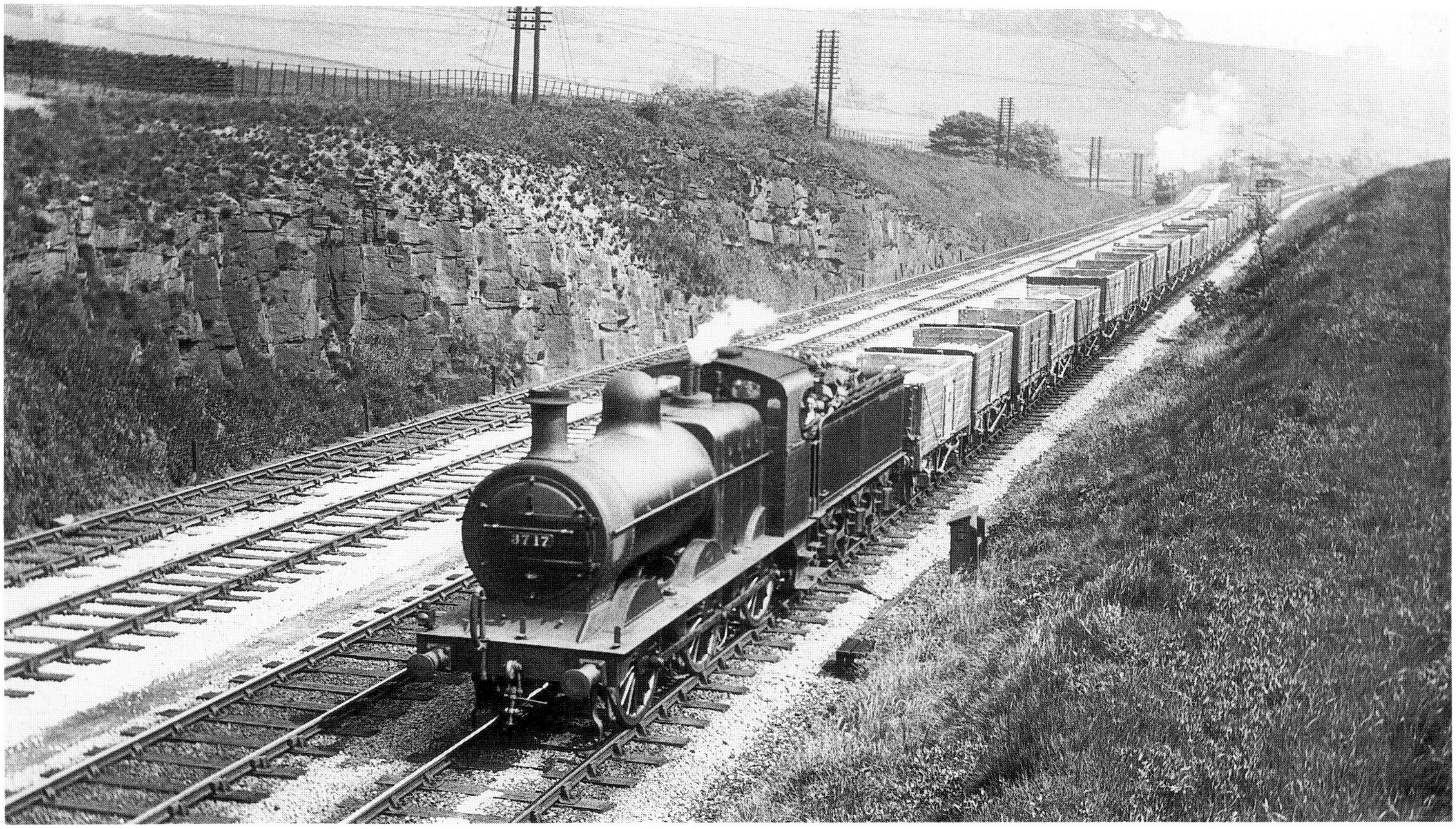

Approach to New Mills South Junction, June 18th.1932: Here we face south towards Buxworth Junction and Chinley. Johnson 0-6-0 of Midland Railway "M" Class, No.**3717** is stationary and, by the looks of things, a re-ballasting operation is in progress. The P.W. engineers will have taken possession of the Fast lines; observe that the side doors of the wagons have been dropped ready for the discharge of ballast. In the shimmering summer haze in the distance, the two sets of lines can be seen to part company revealing the sprawling complex of the Gowhole freight yard. *E.R.Morten*

New Mills South Junction, August 1st.1936: Former Midland Class 2 4-4-0 No.**462** comes along the Up Fast line with a 5-coach stopping train. Notice in the background the junction signal pegged "off" for a Down train to take the "old" route via New Mills. *N.Fields*

New Mills South Junction, September 10th.1932: "Crab" 2-6-0 No.**13136** has been polished to perfection to head this 13-coach special working (coded 651). What a splendid sight this ensemble makes, with its mixture of Midland Clayton and Bain stock, as it passes along the Up Slow line towards Gowhole. *N.Fields*

New Mills South Junction, May 17th.1952: For me no other locomotives epitomise so well the atmosphere of the Manchester-St.Pancras expresses than the "Jubilees." Handsome machines with a myriad of names, yet often running late and looking uncared for, the "Jubilee" somehow said it all. This picture by Brian Green shows No.**45657** *Tyrwhitt* storming up the Fast line from the junction with the 10.00 a.m. (SO) express from Manchester Central to St.Pancras. With 8 coaches behind the tender, all bar one in the famous "blood and custard" livery of the 1950s, this delightful scene has all the magic ingredients of those far-off days. With a bright summer sky, fleecy clouds and an endless procession of trains- what more could one want? As a footnote, "Tyrwhitt" was a rare bird in these parts; soon afterwards, on August 30th., the engine went northwards to Perth where most of its operational career was spent. It returned south to spend the last months of its life at Patricroft. *B.K.B.Green*

Approach to New Mills South Junction, June 18th.1932: On the same day as the picture of No.**3717** was taken, we look across the tracks as another ex-Midland 0-6-0, this time a Neilson Goods with a Deeley cab, No.3233 inches along the Down Slow line with a very long mixed freight. Stock with pre-Group identity can still be seen-GC and NE wagons are present; also we see familiar names such as "Butterley", "Pinxton" and "Cawoods" painted on the once-common private owner wagon. Tarpaulined wagons, loaded wagons, empty wagons, box vans both short and tall-all are there. A slow-moving train with woefully inefficient motive power, but what a splendid sight it all was! *E.R.Morten*

Gowhole

At the curiously-named location of Gowhole, about one and a half miles south of New Mills South Junction, was sited the vast freight complex known as Gowhole Sidings. Stretching for almost 1,000 yards, and terminating at bridge No.119 where Gowhole Lane crossed the line and Buxworth Junction commenced, this was one of the Midland's last great enterprises in the early years of the twentieth century. It is, therefore, quite surprising that so little has been shown or written about it.

Some sidings had existed at Gowhole from before 1875. Their precise location is not known, but we can ascertain that they belonged to Messrs. L& E Hall and that a signalbox existed here to control the traffic. A replacement had been provided in August 1892; this box was re-named "Gowhole Goods Junction" some two months later. A new lever frame was added in 1903 and this second signalbox lasted until December 1920 when a replacement structure was provided.

The area around Gowhole and New Mills, wild, stark and yet very beautiful, had a surprising past that is worth mentioning. The area was the site of several coal mines-features maybe thought akin to the more southern aspects of the Derbyshire landscape or to certain parts of Yorkshire. Although the coal reserves were not abundant, and output had peaked in the latter part of the nineteenth century, the mines in the vicinity were still producing coal as recently as 1941 when the Noon Sun pit, west of Birch Vale, closed. The coming of the railway was responsible for the early demise of some of these small, local pits. The Beard and Bugsworth colliery had closed in 1903 and the Lady Pit and Gowhole Pit a year earlier: it is stated ("The Coal Mines of New Mills"-Derek Brumhead) that with the opening of the Dore and Chinley railway through to Sheffield in 1894, a large quantity of slack coal was transported into the district. This was superior to anything produced in the area and, indeed, cost little more.

The accompanying plan shows the full extent of the arrangement and a detailed description of the actual layout is not really necessary. Passing under bridge No.124, towards Buxworth and Chinley, the running lines split-dividing the complex into two rough halves: the Slow lines took a slightly raised path; to their left, set down below in a north-easterly direction, a series of ten siding roads fanned out. access to these was via a Reception line facing off the Up Slow. Adjacent to the Slow lines was the signalbox and, behind the top row of sidings, engine facilities in the shape of a water crane and a 60 ft. turntable were provided. Passing the signalbox and heading towards Buxworth and Chinley, the main siding complex was set out, again, at a lower level. This arrangement consisted of a set of twelve sidings connected at each end to a lengthy neck. Direct access to these sidings was provided from the Down Slow line.

Below this second part of the complex, the Fast lines ran by, unimpeded by any connection or junction with the yard. Under Gowhole Lane (bridge 119) the Fast and Slow lines came alongside once more. Here was Buxworth Junction where, as at New Mills South, crossings were provided to enable trains to move from Fast to Slow lines and vice-versa in either direction.

Gowhole Sidings, September 5th.1966: A view from the footbridge that spanned the Buxworth end of the yard looking towards New Mills South Junction. At once, the complexity and size of the place is readily taken in. Over to the right an 8F 2-8-0 rumbles past on the Down Slow line with a freight-at least four wagons of which are loaded with ballast. Just glimpsed, over on the extreme left-hand side, are the Fast lines; between these and the passing freight train is the main siding complex set below. Though not completely packed with wagons, the yard still has a busy air about it. Completing the picture is the signalbox, seen just off to the left centre and, of course, the beautiful Derbyshire hills. *A.K.Rathbone*

Gowhole Sidings, September 17th.1961: A view of the Slow lines that passed along the top of the yard with "Scot" No.**46164** *The Artists' Rifleman* at the head of the 11.45 Manchester Central to Chinley. In the background can be seen the signalbox and the fan of ten sidings that were spread out behind the Up and Down Slow lines. To the left, at a lower level, is the main yard layout spanning the ground between here and the Fast lines. The two tracks off to the extreme right were shunting necks which terminated in front of the footbridge (bridge No.121). *Raymond Keeley*

Gowhole Sidings, n.d: The ten sidings roads on the north-eastern side of the line are spread out to the right here with the signalbox just in front. The south end of the main siding complex is visible to the left of the picture with, again, the running lines passing on either side. *Harry Townley*

Gowhole Sidings, n.d: This was the south end of the yard-a shot taken, again, from the footbridge. The misty appearance of the background tends to confirm that this was a wet day. Just entering the shunting neck, engaged in a spot of fly-shunting is Standard Class 4 No.**75060**. From this vantage point can be seen the two separate sets of through lines: Fast lines to the right, Slow lines to the left; these converge just ahead at Buxworth Junction. The little gabled structure just to the centre right is labelled as a "lever hut" whilst in front, on the same side, is a shunters' cabin. *A.K.Rathbone*

Gowhole Sidings, April 4th.1953: 4F No.**44588** has come to a stand on the Up Fast line just alongside bridge No.121. Known as Shirt's Bridge, this was a public footpath carried over the Slow line and sidings and under the Fast lines on the opposite side. Of lattice girder construction, Shirt's Bridge consisted of two main steel truss girders with lattice bracing. Originally built in 1865 to span the original lines (the present Slow Lines) it was lengthened and rebuilt in 1903 to accommodate the new works. Outlasting the yard here, which closed on March 3rd.1969, bridge No.121 survived until the end of May, 1984. *J.D.Darby*

Gowhole Sidings, August 30th.1947: LMS Compound No.**1144** heads the 3.55 p.m. Manchester Central to Chinley train along the Up Fast line. Tucked out of sight below, the central part of the siding complex appears to be full, with wagons and merchandise in abundance.
J.D.Darby

Gowhole Sidings, August 30th.1947: A last look at Gowhole with 4F No.**4536** trundling along the Down Slow line with forty-one empty coal wagons plus the obligatory brake van. In the background the junction Home signals guard the approaches to Buxworth Junction.
R.E.Gee

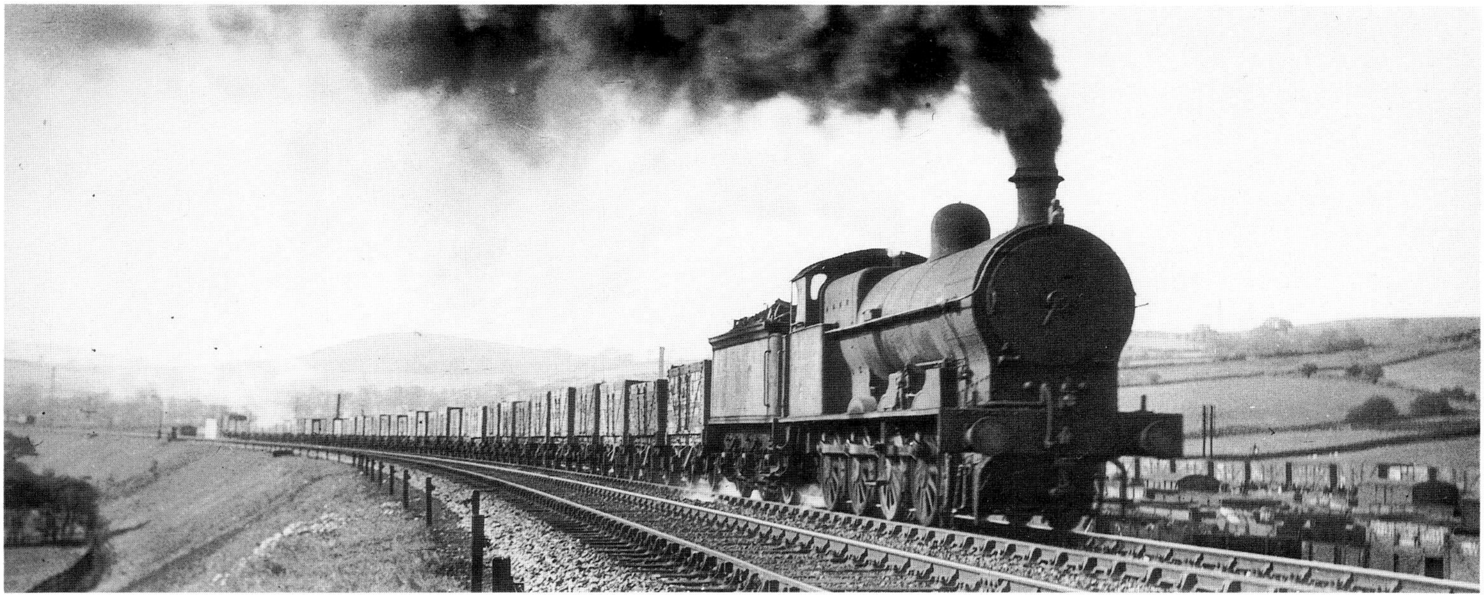

Gowhole Sidings 1945: A brighter day sees an unidentified "Super D" (ex-LNW 0-8-0) pass the yard along the Fast line with an Up train of coal wagon empties. Consisting of some 42 wagons, the sight of such trains underlines the country's dependency on coal at that time.
John Ward

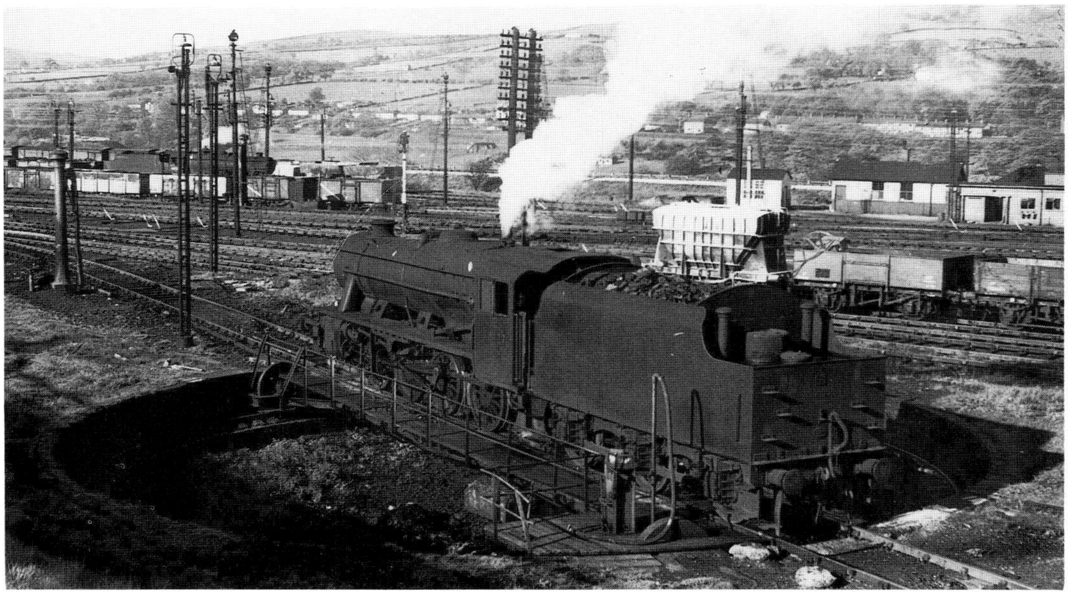

Gowhole Sidings, n.d: 8F No.**48627** stands on the turntable that stood on the north-east side of the complex. The sidings adjacent to the Slow lines come together in the middle foreground.
Harry Townley

Gowhole Sidings, 1945: An almost timeless Midland atmosphere is present here as No.**3425** pulls up the headshunt at the south end of the yard. Livery apart, loco and wooden-bodied wagons are little changed since Victorian times. No.**3425** was built by Messrs.Dubs, to one of Mr.S.W.Johnson's classic designs, in 1892. Many of her compatriots in Midland classes "J" and "J2" were rebuilt with Belpaire fireboxes. Hailing from 19D (Sheffield) No.3425, kept her round-topped boiler until withdrawal. *P. Ward*

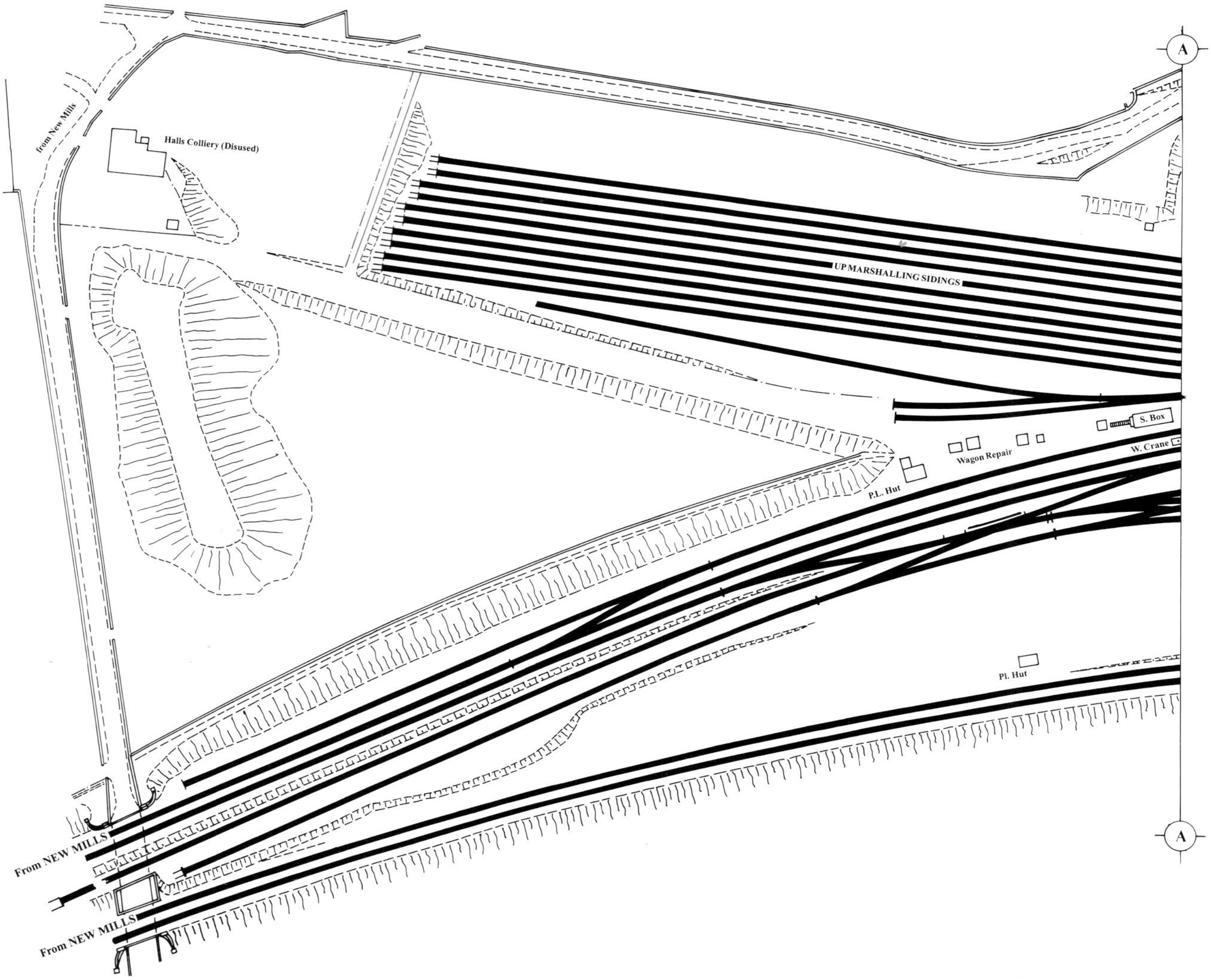
from New Mills
Halls Colliery (Disused)
UP MARSHALLING SIDINGS
S. Box
W. Crane
Wagon Repair
P.L. Hut
Pl. Hut
From NEW MILLS
From NEW MILLS
A
A

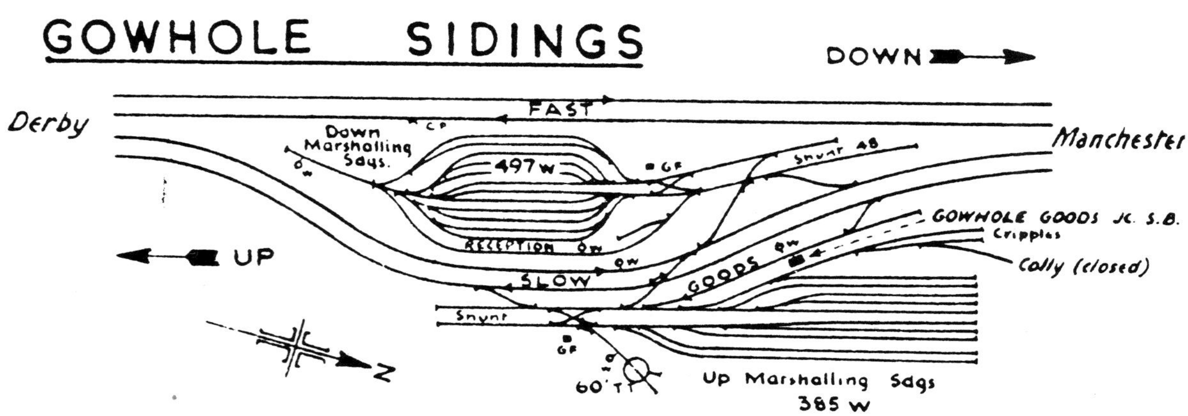
GOWHOLE SIDINGS
DOWN
FAST
Derby
Manchester
Down Marshalling Sdgs.
497 w
GF
Shunt 48
GOWHOLE GOODS Jc. S.B.
Cripples
Colly (closed)
UP
RECEPTION
SLOW
GOODS
Shunt
GF
60' TT
Up Marshalling Sdgs
385 w
N

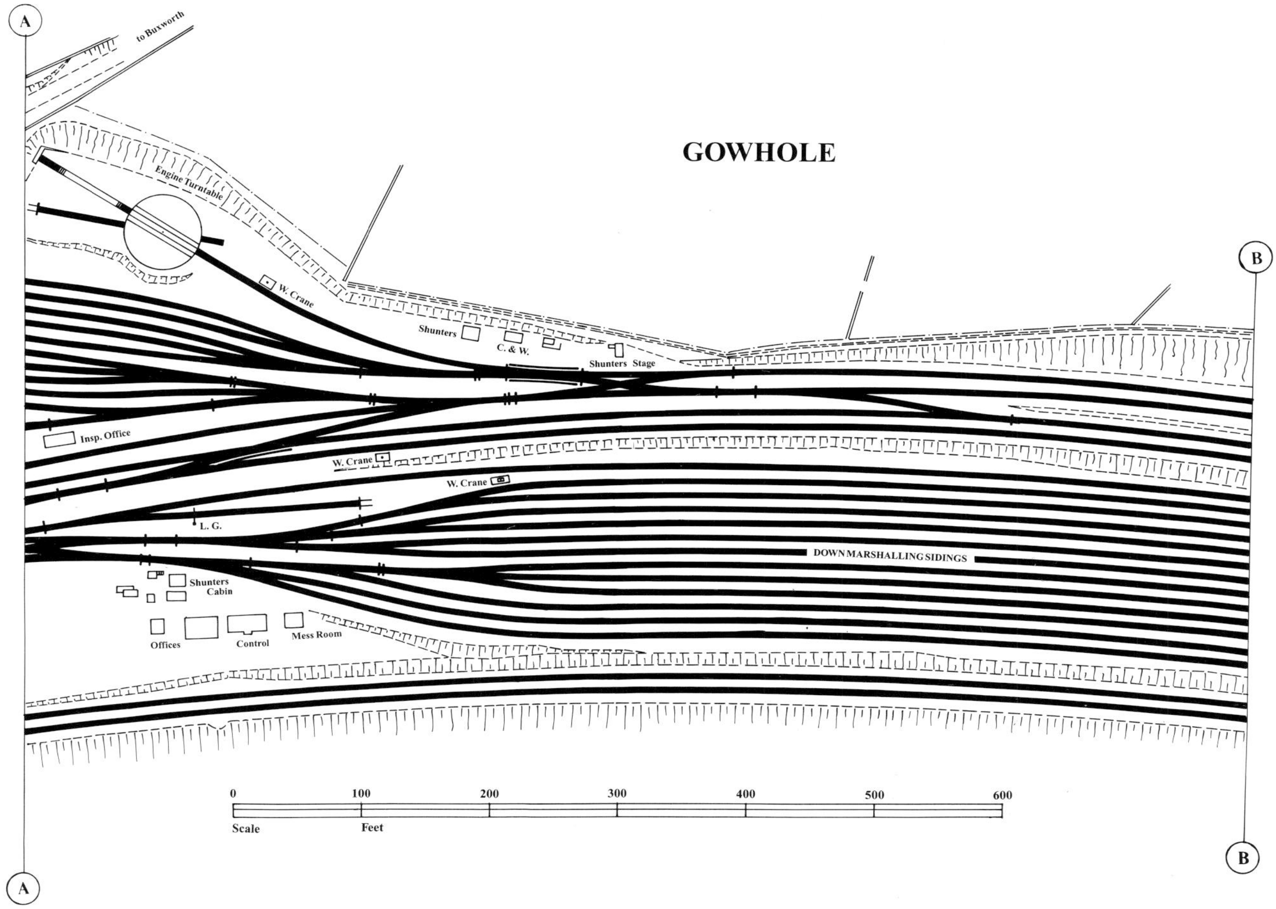
A
to Buxworth
GOWHOLE
Engine Turntable
W. Crane
Shunters
C. & W.
Shunters Stage
B
Insp. Office
W. Crane
W. Crane
L. G.
DOWN MARSHALLING SIDINGS
Shunters Cabin
Offices
Control
Mess Room
0
100
200
300
400
500
600
Scale
Feet
A
B

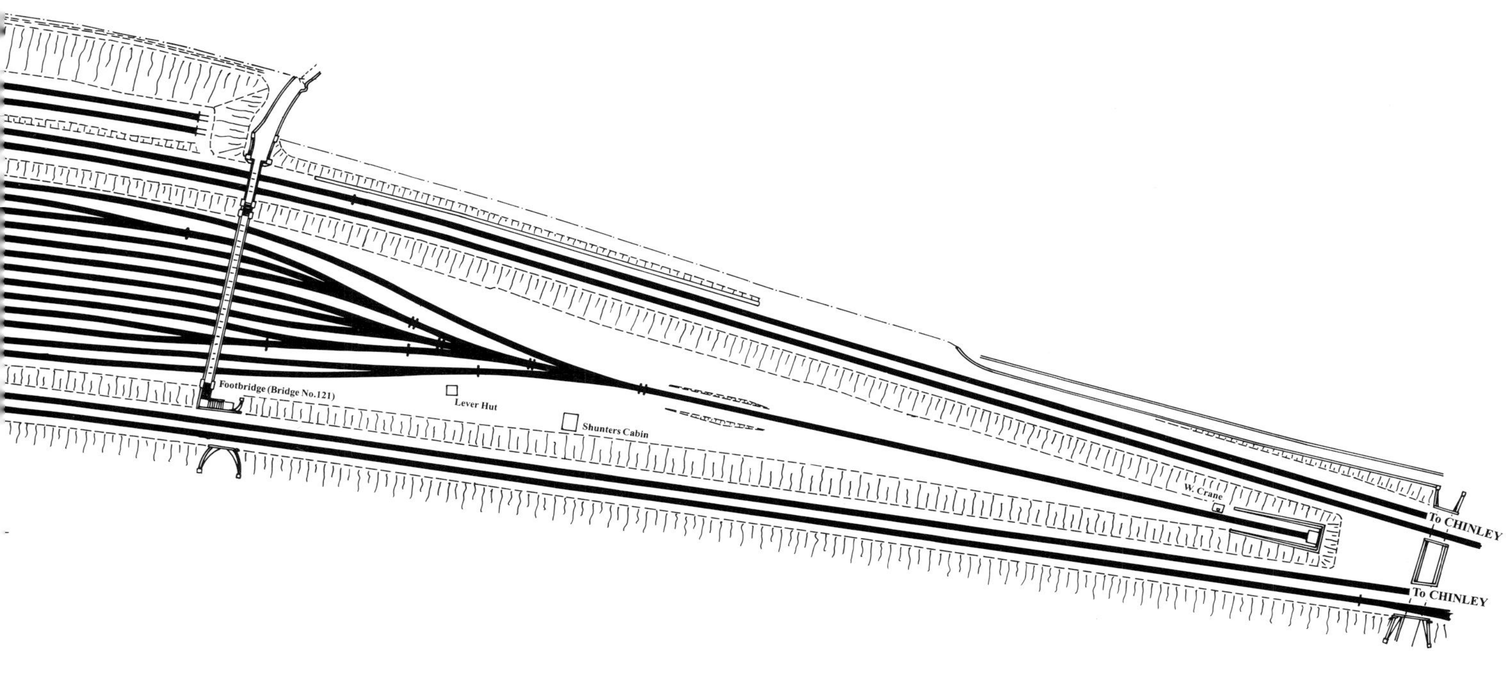
Footbridge (Bridge No.121)
Lever Hut
Shunters Cabin
W. Crane
To CHINLEY
To CHINLEY

Gowhole Sidings, n.d: A feast for all wagon buffs is spread out here in the centre of Gowhole Yard. 8F No. **8493** passes by on the Down Slow line with yet more wooden-bodied wagons. *Harry Townley*

FREIGHT TRAIN AND SHUNTING RECORD-GOWHOLE GOODS JUNCTION

WEDNESDAY, AUGUST 19TH. TO THURSDAY, AUGUST 20TH. 1953

PART 1-From DOWN Sidings

BOOKED DEP. TIME	FROM	TO	DEPARTED ENGINE NO	AT
7.16	Gowhole	Brewery Sidings	90669	7.05
5.23	Peak Forest	Heaton Mersey	48528	8.00
1.40	Kirkley	Trafford Park	48530	10.05
3.05	Avenue Sidings	Gowhole	43211	8.20
8.29	Gowhole	Strines	45135	8.29
9.30	Gowhole	Collyhurst St.	90568	9.30
3.55	Westhouses	Gowhole	48495	8.40
10.00	Gowhole	Brindle Heath	90163	10.00
JOCKO*	Up Side	Down Side	43756	10.02
5.43	Staveley	Gowhole	48341	10.24
JOCKO*	Down Side	Up Side & return	43638	10.25
4.30	Avenue Sidings	Gowhole	47968	11.00
10.40	Gowhole	Heaton Mersey	44327	11.10
2.55	Kirkley	Gowhole	48006	11.15
12.30	Gowhole	Ashton Road	43638	12.10
11.10	Gowhole	Halewood	48101	11.25
7.20	Staveley	Gowhole	48546	11.40
7.05	Rowsley	Gowhole	43081	12.05
9.25	Sheffield	Gowhole	48662	12.55
12.10	Gowhole	Brindle Heath	90376	1.05
Special	Gowhole	Trafford Park	45135	2.20
12.10	Gowhole	Brewery Sidings	90122	2.35
3.10	Gowhole	Heaton Mersey	44179	2.45
10.05	Staveley	Gowhole	44663	2.50
——	Carlton	Gowhole	48113	3.20
4.35	Gowhole	Clifton	43854	4.20
4.20	Gowhole	Heaton Mersey	44179	3.45
6.30	Gowhole	Disley	90163	7.40
7.25	Gowhole	Stuart Street	90404	6.00
12.05	Avenue	Gowhole	43959	5.10
1.10	Not recorded		47973	5.30
2.45	Rowsley	Gowhole	44429	6.55
6.45	Gowhole	Halewood	48135	6.55
——	Sheffield	Gowhole	48652	7.15
Light Engine	Up	Down	43638	7.15
2.15	Avenue Sidings	Gowhole	48682	8.05
——	Down	Up	43756	8.30
3.40	Rowsley	Trafford Park	44168	8.55
——	Gowhole	Ashton Road	90163	9.40
7.20	Gowhole	Heaton Mersey	43945	10.35
6.10	Gowhole	Brindle Heath	43927	10.05
2.45	Westhouses	Gowhole	48057	9.45
8.40	Gowhole	Trafford Park	44168	9.05
1.17	Kirkley	Ashton Road	43970	11.00
11.00	Gowhole	Heaton Mersey	48329	11.35
2.45	Westhouses	Gowhole	48060	11.30
11.20	Gowhole	Ashton Road	43756	11.10
8.10	Earles Sidings	Cheadle	44274	11.00

THURSDAY, 20TH. AUGUST

8.14	Peak Forest	Trafford Park	43836	12.15
4.30	Avenue Sidings	Gowhole	47968	12.30
7.05	Staveley	Gowhole	48210	12.40
8.08	Sheffield	Gowhole	48746	1.10
10.50	Sheffield	Liverpool	48114	2.40

9.00	Rowsley	New Mills	44774	3.15
6.58	Westhouses	Gowhole	48212	2.30
3.40	Gowhole	Trafford Park	48680	5.45
Trip	Gowhole	New Mills	48089	3.15
12.27	Nottingham	Colne	43910	3.30
1.25	Gowhole	Heaton Mersey	48275	4.40
4.35	Gowhole	Liverpool	44179	4.30
3.30	Gowhole	Ancoats	44774	4.15
3.55	Gowhole	Heaton Mersey	48089	4.55
Special	Gowhole	Brindle Heath	44168	5.25
8.30	Kirkley	Gowhole	48383	5.30
9.10	Avenue Sidings	Gowhole	47967	6.00

PART 2-From UP Sidings

BOOKED DEP. TIME	FROM	TO	DEPARTED ENGINE NO.	AT
2.30	Gowhole	Sheffield	4447	7.00
Trip	Shed	Buxworth Jct.	4852	6.52
Trip	Shed	Gowhole	6513	7.25
6.00	Moston	Gowhole	9056	8.25
Special	Gowhole	Avenue	4321	8.30
9.05	Gowhole	Westhouses	4849	9.45
5.45	Philips Park	Gowhole	90163	9.30
6.45	Ashton Road	Gowhole	43736	9.55
5.58	Arpley	Gowhole	44327	10.25
Trip	Down	Up (and return)	43638	11.00
10.25	Gowhole	Staveley	48341	10.45
9.15	Cheadle	Gowhole	48101	11.02
9.40	Gowhole	Avenue Sidings	47968	11.10
9.05	Trafford Park	Peak Forest	43836	2.41
11.00	Gowhole	Rowsley	48006	11.45
11.20	Gowhole	Staveley	48546	12.05
Light Engine	Gowhole	Rowsley	43881	12.20
8.1	Moston	Gowhole	90376	12.57
——	Guide Bridge	Gowhole	90140	1.25
1.28	Gowhole	Sheffield	48662	1.30
9.20	Collyhurst	Gowhole	90122	2.12
Special	Halewood	Gowhole	44119	not rec.
11.20	New Mills	Gowhole	65135	2.10
3.20	Gowhole	Staveley	48663	3.10
1.40	Heaton Mersey	Gowhole	43854	3.25
9.20	Walton	Gowhole	44179	3.40
Light Engine		Gowhole	48113	3.35
2.40	Hollinwood	Gowhole	90404	5.00
1.40	Brindle Heath	Gowhole	90163	5.00
5.10	Gowhole	Avenue Sidings	43959	5.45
4.25	Cheadle	Gowhole	48135	6.15
6.20	Gowhole	Avenue Sidings	47973	6.20
——	Gowhole	Rowsley	44429	7.05
6.45	Ashton Road	Gowhole	43638	7.20
7.50	Gowhole	Sheffield	48652	7.35
——	Gowhole	Avenue Sidings	48682	8.25
7.42	Cheadle(?)	Gowhole	43945	9.00
——	Bredbury	Gowhole	43927	9.00
JOKO*	Down	Up	43756	10.40
——	Shed	Gowhole	90163	9.00
Trafford	Down	Up	44168	9.10
——	Philips Park	Rowsley	43368	9.35
——	Gowhole	Westhouses	48057	10.20
Light Engine	Gowhole	Staveley	48060	11.50
10.40	Ancoats	Rowsley	45031	12.15

Gowhole Sidings, n.d: Here we look from the footbridge towards New Mills South Junction on a scene in LMS days packed with activity. For the moment the Slow lines are quiet, but careful observation shows much going on. In the shunting neck a Hughes/Fowler 0-8-0 is in charge of seventeen wagons, plus a brake van; on the adjacent road more wagons-mostly loaded with coal await their charges. The centre roads, too, are chock-a-block: open wagons-high and low-sided, sheeted wagons, box vans and locomotives in waiting. A once-familiar scene here, now, incredibly, all reduced to nothing. *Harry Townley*

THURSDAY, 20TH.AUGUST

9.35	Gowhole	Avenue Sidings	47968	12.40
11.55	Gowhole	Staveley	48210	1.25
11.20	Trafford Park	Gowhole	48680	2.50
10.55	Gowhole	Sheffield	48746	2.15
11.40	Heaton Mersey	Gowhole	48089	2.50
1.45	Gowhole	Leeds	48654	2.45
11.38	Moston	Rowsley	43628	2.35
Light Engine	Gowhole	Westhouses	48212	3.00
10.55	Walton	Sheffield	44020	4.20
1.30	Trafford Park	Gowhole	44168	4.45

This is an extract from the freight train and shunting record kept at Gowhole Goods Junction signalbox. The full records run to nineteen columns and record, amongst other things, the number of wagons detached and left in the yard, the shunting time and standing time for both the train and the shunting engine, and sundry details such as the duties and meal times taken by the shunting engine crew. The starred item (*) termed "Jocko" or "Joko" is North-West railway vernacular for a shunting engine; at Belle Vue shed, Manchester, the term was used to describe the Midland "Open Cab" or "Half Cab" Johnson 0-6-0 Tank engines. Here we see the term applied to shunting engines which would have had occasion to cross from one side of the yard to the other. Maybe there is some significance in that Belle Vue engines supplied Pilot locomotives for the yard. In 1953, 3F 0-6-0s **43612**, **43638** and **43756** were working these turns.

Motive power in and out of Gowhole shows a good cross-section of London Midland (ex LMS) freight and mixed traffic types. 3F and 4F 0-6-0s, Class 5 4-6-0s, "Crab" 2-6-0s, 8Fs and the popular "Austerity" (ex WD) 2-8-0s were all regular visitors. Although many had been withdrawn by 1953, the occasional 7F 0-8-0 could be seen in the yard, mainly those left at Newton Heath Loco. Notice too, the incidence of the ex-LMS Beyer-Garratt machines on the 4.45 a.m. Avenue Sidings (Chesterfield)-Gowhole trains, returning on the 9.45 a.m. Gowhole-Avenue and also on the 1.10 p.m. Avenue-Gowhole-returning on the 6.10 p.m. Gowhole to Avenue. These turns were usually worked by an 18C Hasland (Chestefield loco).

The 5.58 a.m. Warrington Arpley to Gowhole would, on occasions, bring an LNWR 0-8-0 from 8B (Warrington) shed. This working returned from Gowhole with the 10.40 a.m. to Heaton Mersey Sidings.

In 1953, a working day in the yard would see visits from a vast number of engine sheds. Those which supplied motive power on a regular basis were: 8B (Warrington), 8C (Speke Junction), 9D (Buxton), 9F (Heaton Mersey), 15A (Wellingborough), 16C (Kirkby), 17A (Derby), 17B (Burton), 17D (Rowsley), 18A (Toton), 18B (Westhouses), 18C (Hasland), 18D (Staveley), 19A (Grimesthorpe), 20B (Stourton), 20C Royston), 26A (Newton Heath), 26G (Belle Vue), and 27B (Aintree). Visits would also be made from many of the other Midland Division sheds, but those quoted were the most frequent.

A J10 0-6-0 from Heaton Mersey shed could quite often be seen in the yard working local trips to New Mills and Cheadle Heath sidings. In 1953, **65132**, **65160** and **65178** frequently worked this turn.

Some idea of the complexity of operation and the sheer intensiveness of the traffic coming in and out of the yard can be gleaned by simple observation from the tables summarised above: entry No.3 on the Down sidings shows the train from Kirkley to Trafford Park arriving at 7.35 and spending no less than 2 hours, 5 minutes awaiting a path. Entries 5/6/& 8 from the Down sidings on the same morning were awaiting paths for 39/50 and 25 minutes respectively. Various workings are pencilled as "Waiting Guard" (staff shortages are nothing new!); one hour and two hours, five minutes appearing on several occasions.

On the morning of our observations, no less than thirty trains left Gowhole in the morning period between 7.00 and 12.10 (just into the afternoon). Oddly enough, the departures split exactly 50/50-15 Up and 15 Down. On a general basis, there appears to be, on average, well over 100 movements in and out of the yard on a typical weekday. This is quite apart from the shunting trips, with just over 2,000 wagons being handled in a 24-hour period.

If one takes into consideration the main line and local passenger trains which passed Gowhole on the nearby Fast and Slow lines up and down from Buxworth Junction, then this location would, indeed, be a busy one; providing the observer with a vast variety of locos and train workings and offering a plethora of movements between a very wide range of engine sheds.

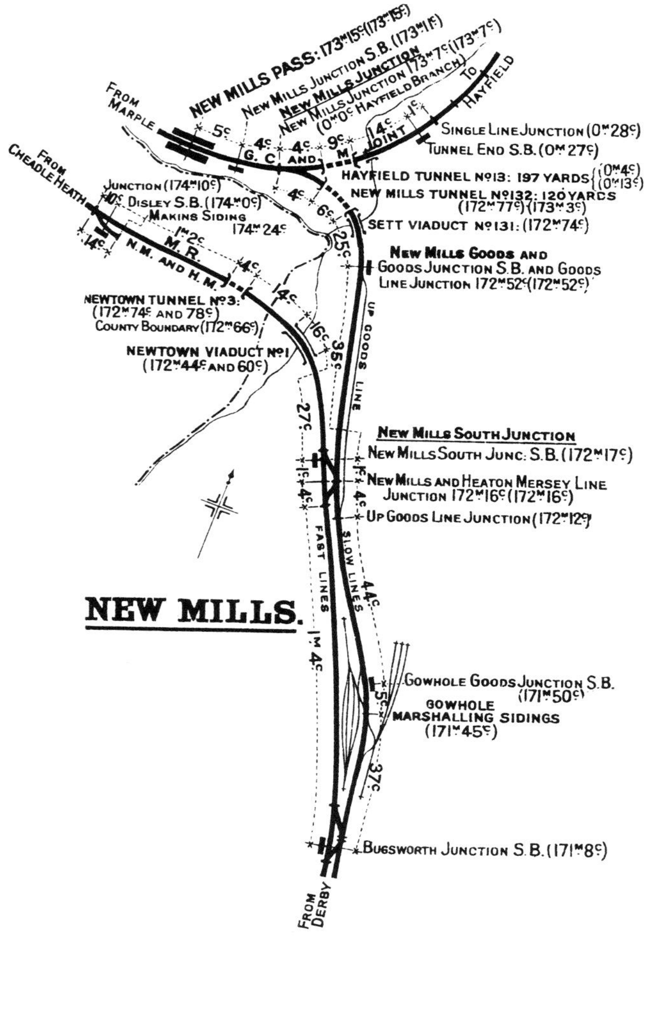

The later 1950s show the yard still busy. Even Christmas Day, when nowadays the whole of the BR system sleeps-save for the odd ICI Hopper train in recent years, Gowhole still managed to drum up some traffic. The big day in 1956 saw twenty freight movements; these were all handled in the early hours of the morning-between Midnight and 4.39 a.m. Thereafter, Gowhole Goods Junction box closed and signalman A.Livesley went off home to open his presents. Boxing Day (a Wednesday) saw no traffic and the box opened for business again at 5.05 a.m. on December 27th. Again, perusal of the train register shows the extent of the freight traffic passing through the complex. The register in question (38 entries per page) has 100 pages and lasts for just the period from Christmas Eve 1956 to February 7th.1957.

Four signalmen appear to have manned the box on a regular basis in those days: W.Green, A.Livesley (who I must commend for his impeccable handwriting!), E.Trillington and A.Jones (possibly a relief man). To peruse a train register from a place like Gowhole is to obtain a glimpse inside the very heart of such an operation. Booking on and off times of the men working the box, visits by linesmen to repair or test equipment, "detaching cripples"-wagons with hot axleboxes (on the afternoon of New Year's Eve), All the entries record a diligence to duty and evidence of sound and methodical training: Signalman Livesley seems to have been particularly attentive as regards his equipment: "light indicators in order" is inked in at the start of each shift; likewise, "electric locks on 37 & 39 and detonator machines in order at noon" are shown in an immaculate hand. Also appearing is "water and relief" on a fairly regular basis and, rather comically, "driver warned of sheep on line" -5.04 on the afternoon of January 25th., signalman Livesley again. The engine concerned was a Garratt (No.47978) on an Up working; the stray animals had been rounded up by 5.29 when the line was recorded as clear.

By dint of studying minutae in records like this, we step back into time and lapse into another world when the railways still played a major part in the movement of the country's freight. The operation of a yard complex such as Gowhole was an immense task, the yard existing at the very hub of freight operations to and from the Midlands and the North-West. It was as far back as 1909 that the Midland Railway first introduced its centralised traffic control system. Under this scheme, Gowhole was designated as one of twenty-five separate divisions for train control purposes. The area covered was large: it extended to Liverpool in the west, almost to Hellifield in the north-east and Chester and Peak Forest in the south-west and south-east respectively. In 1921, along with Saltley, Gowhole was one of the biggest control divisions in an area that covered almost the length and breadth of the country.

One more decade after our records and Gowhole Sidings began to slip into oblivion. Among its many recommendations, the Beeching Report saw no future for single-wagonload freight-which of course had been the bread and butter of places like Gowhole. Co-incident with Beeching was the inexorable advance of the manifestations of the Clean Air Act (1956) which banned the burning of coal in towns and cities. Gradually, the wayside goods yard, a feature of the railway scene from the very early years, began to ebb away. By the time of Beeching too, the railways themselves were abandoning the use of coal as a motive power fuel. The Up Traffic Sidings were closed the week ending March 3rd.1969. Gowhole Goods Junction signalbox closed on May 18th.1969; the Up and Down Sidings ground frames were taken out of use at the same time. Finally, the yard was dismantled between March 12th. and May 3rd.1970. Today, only the former Fast lines remain, traversed by the anonymous, air-conditioned Class 158 units sweeping past en route to and from Sheffield, the East Coast ports and East Anglia. Gowhole Sidings, a freight Mecca in the Derbyshire countryside, have vanished into history.

Gowhole Goods Junction Signalbox, n.d: This was Gowhole's nerve centre, the Goods Junction box. Dating from 1920, it was to Midland period III design-windows on all sides extending down to floor-level. Notice the "usual offices" on the landing by the door, not a typical Midland feature and, almost certainly, a later addition.
Collection of Alan Barnard.

BUXWORTH JUNCTION

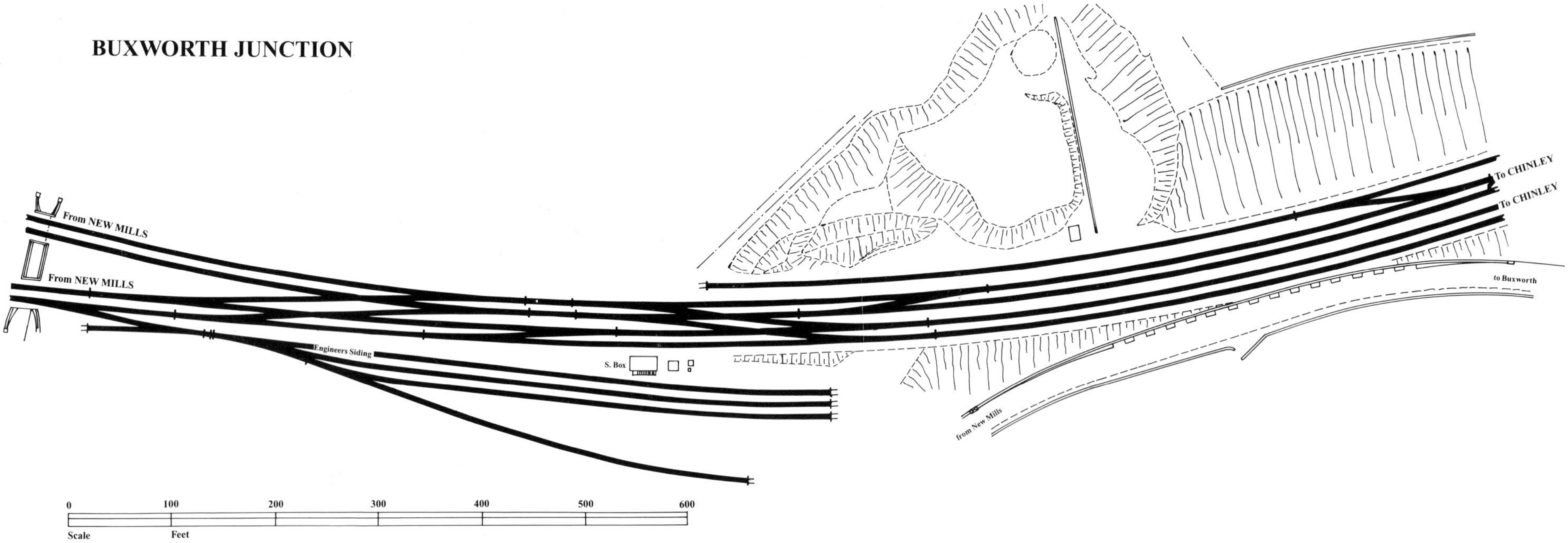

(right). **Buxworth Junction, n.d**: A view from Buxworth Junction signalbox showing "Jubilee" No.**5554** *Ontario* passing the junction with an Up express. Midland signals are apparent in this view; Shirt's Bridge, spanning Gowhole Yard, is visible in the background and a Stanier engine waits at the Home signal for a passage over the junction and on towards Chinley. *Collection of M. Graty*

Approaches to Gowhole, c.1947: Approaching Gowhole from Buxworth is one of the LMS Garratts, No.**7996**. These cumbersome-looking machines were frequently deployed to and from Avenue Sidings, Chesterfield, on freights to Gowhole Yard. *P. Ward*

Gowhole Sidings 1947: A friendly wave from the fireman as "Jubilee" No.**5616** *Malta G.C.* storms along the Up Fast line and ascends the 1-in-90 past the yard and on towards Buxworth Junction and Chinley. The engine is in the short-lived black, lined straw and maroon, LMS Standard livery with block numerals and lettering, first applied in 1946. *P.Ward*

Buxworth Junction, May 2nd.1953: 4F No.**44142**, coupled to a self-weighing tender, is about to take the Up Fast to Up Slow crosssover road at the head of what looks like a train of coal empties. In the box, the "Bobby"-hand on lever frame-watches the proceedings carefully. This typical Midland period III box had opened as "Bugsworth Junction" on May 24th.1903. Housing a 42-lever frame, it closed on October 9th.1966. After removal of the frame, the signalbox shell, complete with floor and rear staircase, but minus roof, was left behind. This provided an excellent, impromptu and strictly unofficial, viewing platform for visiting photographers to the lineside here! *J.D.Darby*

Buxworth Junction, April 15th.1966: A bitterly cold spring day in Derbyshire is witness to a notable event: the last regular rostered Pullman train is passing Buxworth Junction in the shape of the beautiful and meteoric "Midland Pullman." Keith Rathbone had braved the elements to catch this historic moment when he was invited into the warmth of the box to await the arrival of his subject. The "Bobby" on duty bade him to pull back the sliding window, allowing us to share this poignant memory. Just behind the power car of the Pullman can be seen the Slow lines coming up out of Gowhole Yard. Notice the left-hand arm has gone from the signal bracket, denoting the removal of the crossovers here from Slow to Fast lines and vice-versa. *A.K.Rathbone*

.....and there it was, gone: In a whirl of snow, the splendid 6-car train roars up towards The Peak and on to Chinley Station. Notice, again, the missing signal arms and the site of vanished crossover roads. *A.K.Rathbone*

Buxworth Junction, July 6th. 1957: An interesting contrast with our Midland Railway view on page 60 is provided by the appearance of "Jubilee" No.**45650** Blake covering almost the same spot of ground as the "Single". The train is an 8-coach Manchester Central-St.Pancras express. It was at this point here that Buxworth tunnel was situated before being opened out in 1902. *T.Lewis*

Buxworth Junction, Saturday, May 24th.1958: Giving a fine display as it races along the Up Fast towards Chinley is "Jubilee" No.**45575** *Madras*. The train is the 4.25 p.m. Manchester Central to St.Pancras. Unusually at this time, this service did not make its first stop until Derby (reached at 5.40). After a 5-minute pause the following stops were made: Loughborough (6.07), Leicester (6.23), Kettering (6.59), Luton (7.43). Arrival in St.Pancras was at 8.15. (Fridays and Saturdays 8.25). *W.A.Brown*

Buxworth Junction, 18th.September 1965: An interesting perspective at Buxworth showing that most celebrated of North-West "Jubilees" No.**45705** *Seahorse* being buffeted by a fierce tailwind at the head of an LCGB steam special. Entitled ***The High Peak Rail Tour***, and comprising nine ex-Southern Railway coaches, the train had left Waterloo at 8.30 that morning hauled by No.**4472** *Flying Scotsman*. Travelling via Reading, Didcot, Leamington Spa and Oxford, the special had arrived in Birmingham Snow Hill some 40 minutes late. Coming North via Shrewsbury and Crewe, the LNER Pacific had been exchanged for *Seahorse* at Cheadle Heath. In reportedly poor shape, *Seahorse* took the train over the Peak route via Rowsley, Matlock Bath and Ambergate to Derby. At Aston an LMS Class 5 took the train as far as Leamington where two "Granges" were coupled on for the final leg back to London, arriving at Paddington just under two and a half hours late, putting the finishing touches to a memorable day out for all concerned. Buxworth Junction box can be feintly discerned in the background, while to the far left of the picture can be seen the B6062 road leading off the A6 at Bridgemont to Chinley. Visible here is part of the massive blue-brick retaining wall built to contain the land for the widened line from New Mills South Junction to Chinley. *Martin Welch*

Buxworth Junction, May 24th.1958: Another look at passenger operations at Buxworth sees LMS Compound No.**41165** on the Up Fast line with the 4.03 p.m. Manchester Central to Sheffield stopping train. A fairly pedestrian affair, the 4.03 was typical of stopping or local services over the beautiful "Hope Valley" line in the 1950s. An "all stations " service, the train travelled the "old" route via Tiviot Dale and reached Chinley at 5.15. Calling then at Edale, Hope, Bamford, Hathersage, Grindleford, Dore and Totley, Beauchief, Millhouses and Eccleshall and Heeley, arrival in Sheffield Midland was at 6.16. 2 hours, 13 minutes for the 45½ miles gave an average speed of just 18.4 miles an hour! *W.A.Brown*

Buxworth Junction, July 5th.1958: 4F No.**44013** (just for a change, one of the Midland series from 1911) blasts its way along the Up Slow line with a lengthy freight. The two vans behind the tender were used to bring oranges from Seville, Spain, to Ashburys for Messrs. Robertson's (of Droylsden, Manchester) famous "Golden Shred" marmalade. *W.A.Brown*

Buxworth Junction, n.d: An unusual view in Midland days showing what might be termed the "classic" pre-Group mixed goods train. To paraphrase a well-known daily newspaper- "all freight life is there": tarpaulined wagons, tank wagons, loaded coal wagons, flat wagons and box vans, plus, of course, the essential brake van. A bonus is provided by the sight of a rebuilt Johnson 4-4-0, No.**352** of the "1562" class, as the pilot engine; a Class "M" 0-6-0, No.**3749**, built by Neilsons is the train engine. Under gentle steam, the ensemble is drifting down the grade towards the junction. *Author's collection*

Buxworth

Speeding out of Chinley on board a Manchester-bound express in the 1950s the young enthusiast took little notice of the small, rather seedy-looking, station buildings a little way out of Chinley. I think we'd heard of a place called Buxworth, but that was about all. Anyway, all was passed by in a flash as the train accelerated down the falling gradient towards New Mills South Junction before entering the gloomy confines of Disley Tunnel. A station had existed at Buxworth from early days, opening on February 1st.1867. When the line was widened from New Mills to Chinley in the early years of the century, it was necessary to open out the 264 yard-long tunnel just beyond the station and to provide, in lieu, a deep cutting. This was a massive job: perusal of the Midland Railway's civil engineering drawings shows the opening divided into five sections for operational purposes. The last two parts of the cutting required the removal of 389,965 and 1,600 cubic yards of earth respectively. Work began on September 30th 1901 with the construction of a culvert 3' 0" in diameter. Spoil removal commenced on October 2nd. and by May 10th 1902 the tunnel lining had been reached. Bugsworth tunnel appears to have been removed in four stages commencing on June 15th with the work to be completed by July 13th. The target date for completion of all the work at Buxworth is shown as November 15th 1902. It was here that the landslip trauma occurred in 1866 that so delayed the opening of the line. When the tunnel at Buxworth was being driven, the mouth collapsed, almost suffocating the entombed workers; a place of misfortune indeed. Some ambiguity has arisen concerning the name "Buxworth." When the line was opened the village was named "Bugsworth" and this was in use until 1930. It would seem that the inhabitants of Buxworth were unhappy at the name their place of abode bore. So, on June 4th.of that year, at their request, the station assumed the title "Buxworth." It had been rumoured in recent times that the local worthies wanted the name changed back to its historically correct version. As far as the railway goes this would be purely academic, as both station and junction have now long gone. Buxworth Junction was not a junction in the sense of two diverging routes, but was provided to enable trains in either direction to cross to or from the Slow to Fast lines or vice-versa. Buxworth tunnel had been situated on the south side of the junction. Leaving the site of the junction heading north, the Fast and Slow lines parted company either side of Gowhole Yard. Buxworth Station, serving the Fast lines only, was positioned on the Chinley (south) side of the tunnel. Completing the layout at Buxworth was a set of four sidings on the west side of the line and a single siding, accessed from a trailing crossover on the Up Slow line, on the east side.

Buxworth Tunnel, 1902: Railway operation changes over the years; tracks are widened or electrified, roads diverted and, in consequence, vital parts of the infrastructure such as tunnels have to be removed. When the works from Chinley, south to New Mills, were being undertaken in the early years of the century the Midland Railway opened out the 264 yard tunnel at Buxworth as a consequence of the widening to accommodate quadruple track. The work was in an advanced stage of completion when the contractors posed for the camera enabling this historic moment to be captured on film, or more correctly, plate. The steam crane on the right has been busy and only the remaining section of the north end of the tunnel, along with the lower part of the lining, are left to be dealt with. No doubt as soon as the photographer had finished his work the bowler-hatted foreman, standing just to the right of the crane, will see to it that the men in his charge finish theirs! *Collection of D.Ibbotson*

Buxworth Junction, c.1920: The Johnson "Single" had epitomised all the grace and beauty of the Victorian steam locomotive. Though slightly disfigured in their later years by Deeley's smokebox door and chimney, the original splendour of these superb machines is still manifest in this view as No.**620**, in sparkling condition, leaves the junction behind and runs along the Up Fast line towards towards Chinley with a 5-coach express. *Collection of W.A.Brown*

Buxworth Junction, May 24th.1958: Ascending a 1-in-96 gradient was one thing, descending it, with only a steam-braked locomotive and a guard's van, was quite another. G2 0-8-0 No.**49368** is taking the Down Fast line on the approach to the junction with a lengthy coal train. A cloud of brake dust issuing from the brake van suggests the downhill gradient is giving the guard a run for his money! Note the well worn cess which acted also as a footpath in the days before mechanized track maintenance became the norm. *W.A.Brown*

Buxworth Junction, June 28th.1952: 8F No.**48098** literally slogs along the Up Slow line towards Chinley North Station Junction with a lengthy train of vans. The track on the right was a single siding which paralleled the Slow lines. *B.K.B.Green*

Buxworth Station, Saturday September 29th.1956: 8F No.**48254**, a Northwich (9G) engine takes a cautious approach to Gowhole Goods Junction whilst in charge of a Down Class D Hopper train. Officialdom designated these trains to be signalled on the block bell with five consecutive beats classifying them as: "express freight, livestock, perishable or ballast train, partly fitted with the automatic brake operative on not less than one third of the vehicles." *Norman Jones*

Buxworth Station, June 28th.1952: Buxworth Station was situated on the Fast lines and does not seem to have attracted the attention of many photographers. Passing along the Up Slow at the back of the station is G2 0-8-0 No.**49149** with a mineral empties. Buxworth's Up platform can be seen, bordered by characteristic Midland-pattern slatted fencing. Still lit by oil, the platform sported little more than a wooden waiting shelter in terms of passenger facilities. *B.K.B.Green*

Buxworth Station, May 17th.1952: Seven coaches are behind the tender of "Jubilee" No.**45561** *Saskatchewan*-a Bristol (Barrow Road) engine-as it clears Buxworth Station and heads along the Up Fast line in the direction of Chinley. Just this side of the station can be glimpsed the splitting Distants for the junction ahead. Sprouting from behind the train are the Chinley Station North Junction Up Distants-this well-known location now being around three-quarters of a mile away. *B.K.B.Green*

Between Buxworth and Chinley, n.d: A dramatic and yet quite stark winter scene set in slightly more modern times as we look across the Down Fast line towards the remains of Buxworth Station. 8F No.**48775** charges along the Up Slow and ascends the 1-in-96 gradient with a mixed freight-probably just out of Gowhole. The engine is just crossing one of the two underbridges required here in a relatively short distance to accommodate the B6062 road as it weaves its way beneath the railway on its passage from the A6 towards Chinley. The building behind the tree with rather ecclesiastical lines is a school in Buxworth village. Sited between Brierley Park and Brierley Green and dated 1826, a memorial tablet set in the wall reads "pro bono publico." *Martin Welch*

Chinley Station North Junction July 1957: An excellent view of the quadrupled approach to Chinley Station is provided by this picture, taken to record the re-signalling in progress in the Summer of 1957. A standard steel tubular post signal has been erected in the middle of the Fast and Slow lines to replace the wooden affair on the right. Set on the "wrong" side of the line, this signal, with its LMS-pattern corrugated steel arms, is similar to the one we saw at New Mills South Junction. In front of the overbridge the splendid Midland Railway bracket signal is giving way to a single post affair. Splitting Distants (the one seen is for Chinley Station Junction South) were then falling out of favour with the S&T Department. Spanning the junction is bridge No.113. With stone abutments and lattice steelwork, it was known as "Co-Operative Bridge." Erected originally in 1865, it was rebuilt when the 1903 widening was in progress.
T.Lewis

Chinley Station North Junction, July 17th.1966: Here we have walked forward and are standing on bridge No.113. Looking towards Buxworth we notice that the new signals have long been in place; Chinley Station South Junction's Up Fast Distant is "off" as Type "4" Diesel No.**D155** clears the double spans of Broadhurt's bridge (No.114) and runs through the junction prior to entering Chinley Station. The train, a 6-coach formation, is a stopping train to Derby.
T.Lewis

Chinley

The history of railways is punctuated by the development and growth of places which owe virtually all such abundance to the coming of this particular form of transport. Crewe, of course, is a prime example, another might be Woodford Halse;Highbridge, Melton Constable, Swindon and Horwich are names, too, which spring readily to mind from the fount of railway growth. Thus, finally, we alight at Chinley. Not, certainly, a railway "town" by any means, but a place, nevertheless, where one railway system at least had a definite focus. We saw earlier on of how Marple had grown from a single-line, one platform affair to a busy through station with goods, ample passenger and even locomotive facilities. Hemmed in by its geography though, expansion and development here were, not to say the least, difficult. The Midland Railway had been targetting (to use a piece of current business jargon) the North West of England since the early 1860s. By a process of steady development they had expanded their empire north towards Manchester and west to Liverpool. On 28th.July 1884 the Dore and Chinley Railway was incorporated for a 20½ mile line to run from Dronfield and Dore to Glossop. The following year, powers were obtained to take the line instead through the Peak to Chinley. This had necessitated raising a further £26,000 capital over and above the amount of £1,050,000 with loans of £350,000 originally authorised. Finally, in the summer of 1894, the Dore and Chinley line opened for passenger traffic, connecting the company's interests in the north-west to the steel-making city of Sheffield on the other side of the Pennines. Powers had already been sought to build the New Mills and Heaton Mersey line when it became apparent that further work would be needed in order to ease the burden on traffic passing through Chinley, especially on the freight side, a direct result of the opening of the line to Sheffield. Thus was enacted the Chinley and New Mills Widening Act of 1900. Quadruple track would be provided (as we have already seen) between New Mills South Junction and Chinley North Junction. At Chinley itself a completely new and vastly enlarged station would be constructed about a quarter of a mile west of the original-a fairly insignificant affair with just two platforms. Its replacement, with five through platform faces, plus a bay at the east end primarily for Derby and Sheffield-bound traffic, was to be a busy station indeed. Junctions either side of the station complex were provided, together with a triangular junction a short distance to the south. Here, traffic from the Dore and Chinley line could transfer to the Derby line southwards, thus avoiding Chinley altogether. Enlarged goods facilities with engine turning and watering arrangements completed the picture. Overseeing and controlling the running of all this were no less than five signalboxes. Truly, a place to be wondered at.

Chinley Station North Junction, n.d: We stand on the shallow grassy bank by the Up Slow line to gaze on Chinley in this introductory view. Looking south-east, across the station area, one of the LMS Garratts built in 1927 crosses the Fast to Slow line crossovers with a train of empty coal wagons en route for the sorting sidings at Gowhole. Chinley was a place of character; it was a focus of operations for the Midland south-east of Manchester and Stockport. It was rich in variety of operation: local services both passenger and freight, main line trains-to Derby, Sheffield, Liverpool, Nottingham and London; all passed through Chinley, a great many stopped there. Heavy freight was in abundance, as our pictures will show. Vast quantities of bulk-especially coal and limestone were transported, night and day, through its six platforms. Raw fuel and material to provide for the myriad of industries that existed in the north-west at one time. A railway gemstone, set in the crown of the beautiful Peak District, this was Chinley. *Eric Oldham*

Chinley Station North Junction, Saturday, September 29th.1956: Greg Fox once told me that his idea of the perfect railway book would be one in whicl no pictures of trains appeared! Only 8F No.**48533** from Wellingborough (15A), waiting for the road alongside platform 5 with a Down coal empties, sullie this view as we take in the whole of Station North Junction from alongside the Up Slow line. A superb example of the work of the master photographer, thi picture truly espouses "the railway in the landscape," something made easier by the sheer breathtaking beauty of the surroundings. Station North Junction bo appears over on the far right: housing a 32-lever frame, 28 of which were operational, the box was opened on June 22nd.1902. Built to a standard Midlan period III design, exhibiting glazing down to floor-level on both sides and front, it was a notable survivor here long after rationalisation and had been earmarke for preservation. (Q.V.) *Norman Jone*

Chinley Station North Junction, May 17th.1952: Thirty years on the Midland Railway has been absorbed into the LMS which, in turn, has become par of British Railways. Nevertheless, the location hasn't changed, Midland appendages and motive power (in ancestry at least) are still the order of the day an the freights are still the same loose-coupled workings with wooden-bodied coal wagons. Hiding at the top of the headshunt on the far side of the picture i on of the Midland's superb clerestory coaches. 4F No.**43995**, in cleaner than usual condition, is on the Up Slow, again with coal empties. In the backgroun can be seen the lattice steelwork of Co-Operative bridge, spanning the tracks in front of the bracket signal. *B.K.B.Green*

Chinley Station North Junction, September 29th.1956: Now we have crossed the line and are standing at the top of the grassy bank alongside the headshunt that ran from the sidings situated behind platform 6. We are facing due east here; once through the station the line curved away to the south-east towards Chinley North Junction. Looking down towards the station a good view of the buildings, platforms and footbridge can be gleaned. In the background, Chinley Head dominates the landscape with Mount Famine behind. The 8F now has the road down to Buxworth, fleeces of steam from the chimney complementing those of the clouds above. *Norman Jones*

Chinley Station North Junction, June 8th.1963: Away from freight to passenger working and, by way of a change, to a non-LMS engine! B1 No.**61004** has come over the Hope Valley line with a stopping train from Sheffield. Pulling away from platform 2 the train is taking the Down Slow to Down Fast crossover road before heading towards Buxworth Junction. Another B1 stands over by the signalbox and an Up freight rumbles through on the Slow line towards Station South Junction. *W.A.Brown*

Chinley Station North Junction. 17th May 1952. The gallows signal at the end of platform 4 beckons "off" as Jubilee No.**45665** *Lord Rutherford of Nelson* - a Kentish Town engine - pulls away from the north end of Chinley station with a Down express. This is the last stage in the 195 mile journey from St.Pancras and with the Peak District behind, it is downhill all the way to Manchester. Another 19 miles or so and Throstle Nest, Castleford Viaduct, the spire of the town hall, and Manchester Central will progressively come into view. Meanwhile, platform 5 plays host to a shortly to depart train which will have provided cross platform connection for north bound travellers heading for Marple, Romiley, Stockport Tiviot Dale and the like. *B.K.B. Green*

Chinley Station North Junction, n.d: Relatively few pictures exist on this stretch of line of that most celebrated pair of Diesels, Nos.10000 and 10001. Here, the second of the duo, No.**10001** dating from the summer of 1948, pulls away from Station Junction North with an express from Manchester. Looking at the pristine state of this historic locomotive, it would be a fair assumption that the engine is undergoing running-in after an overhaul at Derby Works.

Frank Coupland

Chinley Station Yard, March 1958: "Jubilee" No.**45598** *Basutoland* bloodied and unbowed after hitting the rear of the Derby to Manchester train whilst heading a returning Football Special from Luton on the night of March 8th. Despite the quite severe damage, 45598 was repaired and returned to traffic. The crippled engine appears to be providing something of an attraction for at least one family; strange how anachronistic the fashions of 35 years ago look now! *Frank Coupland*

Chinley Station North Junction. n.d. Former Midland Compound No.**41016** seems to be the centre of a spot of bother after a derailment at Chinley. The instance was sufficiently serious to warrant calling out the Gorton breakdown crane: the mess van at the front is an ex-ECJS Clerestory; the rear mess coach is a former Great Central vehicle. Some details of the crane itself are worthy of recording: it was built by Ransomes and Rapier to an order of the Ministry of Supply in 1945; the same design had been built for both the Southern and Great Western railways. Supplied to the LNER and allocated to Gorton, it was numbered 122 becoming DE330122 in 1948. It was further re-numbered RS 1083/45 in 1960. Upon closure of Gorton, the crane was re-allocated to Newton heath in 1965. It migrated south in November 1981 when it was sold to the Bluebell Railway. The fate of No.41016 is less certain; it is not known whether the engine was irreparably damaged in the incident here, but following the derailment No.41016 was withdrawn from traffic, in the week ending October 27th 1951. *Frank Coupland.*

Chinley Station, 1922: The days when Midland engines, even freight workhorses like these, were painted in the beautiful Crimson Lake, are long gone in this picture. Taken in the twilight of the Midland's existence we see two 0-6-0 goods engines: one of Kirtley's curved-frame designs piloting a Johnson 0-6-0 with a Deeley cab. Both engines, each carrying Deeley's distinctive smokebox and chimney, look work-stained and dirty-a condition that befits their duty: another train in the incessant procession of coal workings that plodded back and forth over the Pennines and were so much the lifeblood of this line. Looking beyond the train we see the now familiar Midland semaphores at the end of platform 2 and, partly obscured by the leading engine, one of the company's distinctive angled "running-in" boards bearing the name of the station.
Railway Revivals collection

Chinley Station North Junction, 1922: A re-boilered Johnson 0-6-0 goods engine, number unknown, moves its train of empty coal wagons over the junction and away along the Up Slow line towards the station. *Railway Revivals collection*

Chinley Station Yard, May 1922: Rebuilt Johnson 4-4-0 No.**306** is standing at the end of the approach that led to the turntable road and cattle dock. Carrying "express" lights the engine will prpobably be waiting to take over a Liverpool or Manchester Victoria/Blackburn portion of a train from St.Pancras that will be divided here. To the left, out of sight, is the loop line that passed behind platform 6. Beyond the clerestory coach standing by the turntable is the Chinley Road overbridge, No.112.
Railway Revivals collection

Chinley Station, 1960: To look at the other end of the two-storey building on platforms 2,3 and 4 we cross to the southern-most of the platforms and stand on the edge of platform 5 which served the Down Fast line. It was here, on the night of Saturday, March 8th.1958, that Chinley saw one of its sequence of accidents-something the place seems to have been strangely afflicted with over the years. The 5.15 p.m. Football excursion from Luton to Manchester Central was wrongly admitted under clear signals on the Down Fast line into the station where it ran into the back of the 7.10 p.m. passenger train from Derby to Manchester. On what was a bitterly cold night, the Chinley Station South Junction Down Fast Home signal wire had become fast in frozen clay in a cess where it ran under the track- its failure to return to danger having been overlooked by the signalman. Fortunately, no serious casualties resulted from this, one of five accidents here-in 1904/1958/1978/1986 and 1987. Across to our right is the accommodation on platform 1 which served the Up Slow line. Originally comprising a foremens' room and a gentlemens' first class waiting room, it differed from the other platform buildings in being constructed entirely out of stone.
D.Ibbotson

Chinley, Station Entrance, July 7th.1970: The inauspicious entrance to the station, viewed from Station Road, was in stark contrast to the extensive and fairly lavish facilities provided on the platforms. This reflected, of course, the fact that most of the traffic here was of an interchange nature. By today's standards, car parking at Chinley in 1970 was generously provided for. An interesting slice of social history is obtained by looking at the vehicles parked by the passengers of two decades ago: a Wolseley 16/60, a Ford Anglia, the Humber Sceptre and the Morris Traveller. The station footbridge was one of the last remaining features at Chinley, being dismantled on a piecemeal basis before final removal in September 1990. Its replacement was the structure recovered from Royton Junction. *A. Redway*

Chinley Station, April 4th.1963: B1 No.**61370** rests at platform 1, on the Down Slow line, after bringing the 4.31 from Sheffield over the Hope Valley line. Notice the stone base to the platform buildings with timber superstructure. The platform canopies were of a pattern not dissimilar to those used by the LNWR and were certainly not typically Midland. Great Yarmouth is advertised as an attraction to tempt potential holidaymakers. Remember this is a piece of social history now, these were days when holidays abroad were by no means as commonplace as they are today.
W.A.Brown

Chinley Station, n.d: Taken from the middle of the island platform, with the bay at the far end that was positioned in between the Fast and Slow lines, we are looking towards Station Junction South. On our left is platform 2 serving the Down Slow, to the right platform 4 serving the Up Fast. Ahead, behind the main buildings is the bay platform, number 3. The main building on this island platform was the two-storey affair seen here. A timber-framed and panelled upper storey connecting with the footbridge housed the booking hall and booking and parcels office. Below, at platform-level, and constructed in brick, was the Stationmaster's office and porters' room.
G.H.Platt

Chinley Station, July 7th.1970: A good, general view of the station layout with not a train in sight. The photographer is stood amidst the grassy bank above platform 1 and has pointed his camera northwards. Notice, in particular, the bay platform-numbered 4-and the vast width of the station footbridge.
A.Redway

Chinley Station South Junction. n.d. We looked on a bleak winter's scene at Disley and remarked then on the sometimes atrocious Peak District weather. Taken from the north side of the signalbox, this was Chinley in the grip of that arch-enemy - snow. Alongside platform four, a train departs for the south; the bay platform is almost packed up to platform level and the Slow lines have all but disappeared. A Trilby-hatted figure is about to cross the Down Slow line, probably an Inspector in a state of despair as to how things will work out today. But railwaymen at Chinley were hardy individuals, well-suited to nature's capriciousness. Norman Birkett, a one-time Inspector there recounted to me how, on one occasion, a train of wagons was being set back into the yard in the dark in thick falling snow. Such was the density of the snow underfoot, that several wagons became derailed, the wheels running up and over the rail surface. Not until the snow had thawed, and an attempt to free the wagons made, was the incident discovered! *Frank Coupland.*

Chinley Station, 1960: From platform 2 the object of our attention here is the station footbridge. Spanning all six platforms and the two loop lines the structure had three spans: 51'-9", 50'-0" and 62'-6". Across to our left is platform 1, Chinley Station Junction South signalbox is seen in the distance. *D.Ibbotson*

Chinley Station. 1954. LMS Compound 4-4-0 No.**41163** simmers alongside platform 1 at the head of a stopping train bound over the Slow (Sheffield) lines. The four-coach train exhibits no remarkable features; but I thought the view, with the two animated loco crew, the Midland gas lamp and the sunny surroundings, had a charm and clarity that made me want to share it with readers. What better reason could there be?
P. Ward.

Chinley, south end of Station, June 4th.1950: A scene showing much of interest, especially for those with an eye for ephemera. These fine shunting signals kept a watchful eye on operations at the south end of the yard, just in front of the turntable. Of Midland design, the arms were shallower in depth than running line signals-7" compared to 10" and were 30" from end to pivot (48" for running line). Across from platform 5, beside the left-hand signal, are the Down Outside, Straight Road and Warehouse Roads. Worthy of mention are the Midland's famous angled "running-in" boards carrying the station's name. Station South Junction box shows clearly, with 48 levers, this was the largest of the five Chinley signalboxes. Class 5 No.**44822** waits at platform 4 with an Up passenger train. *J.D.Darby*

Chinley Station South Junction, May 19th.1951: From the end of platform 5 we look towards the Chinley Road overbridge with the "stop end" roads of the turntable and sidings to our right. Approaching on the Down Fast line is G2 0-8-0 No.**49249** with a train of wagon empties. Notice the semaphores beyond the overbridge: the lower arms control entry to the Down Outside Road alongside platform 6 just to our right. *W.J.Skillern*

Chinley Station South end. n.d. As a change from pictures of the more normal passenger and freight trains, I thought a little relief might be welcome. To this end, here is a picture of part of a re-ballasting operation in full swing. Photographed from Chinley Station South box, with a plentiful supply of manual labour in evidence, spent ballast is being shovelled laboriously out from between the tracks and into drop-sided wagons. Perhaps this might be a suitable moment to pay a small tribute to permanent way staff: often only glimpsed by passengers, and frequently operating at times when other mortals are asleep - these are the men upon whom the safe passage of all rail traffic depends.
Frank Coupland

Chinley Station, 1966: Taken from platform 6, this picture shows the opposite side of the footbridge leading down to a point outside the station. Chinley, in a similar way to Crewe and Trent, was more of an interchange station than anything else. This would account for the rather unpretentious approach, nothing grander than a mirror image of the exit from platform 1 was provided for the local populace! 1966 was the year that spelt doom for Chinley, the LM authorities having decided to concentrate all their Manchester-London resources on the newly electrified LNWR main line via Crewe and Stoke-on-Trent. Evidence of creeping disuse can be clearly seen: the goods warehouse is out of use and the siding road into it has been cut back. The two bracket signals controlling movements from the yard have had their arms removed, weeds proliferate amongst the sidings-a steady process of decline has set in. *D.Ibbotson*

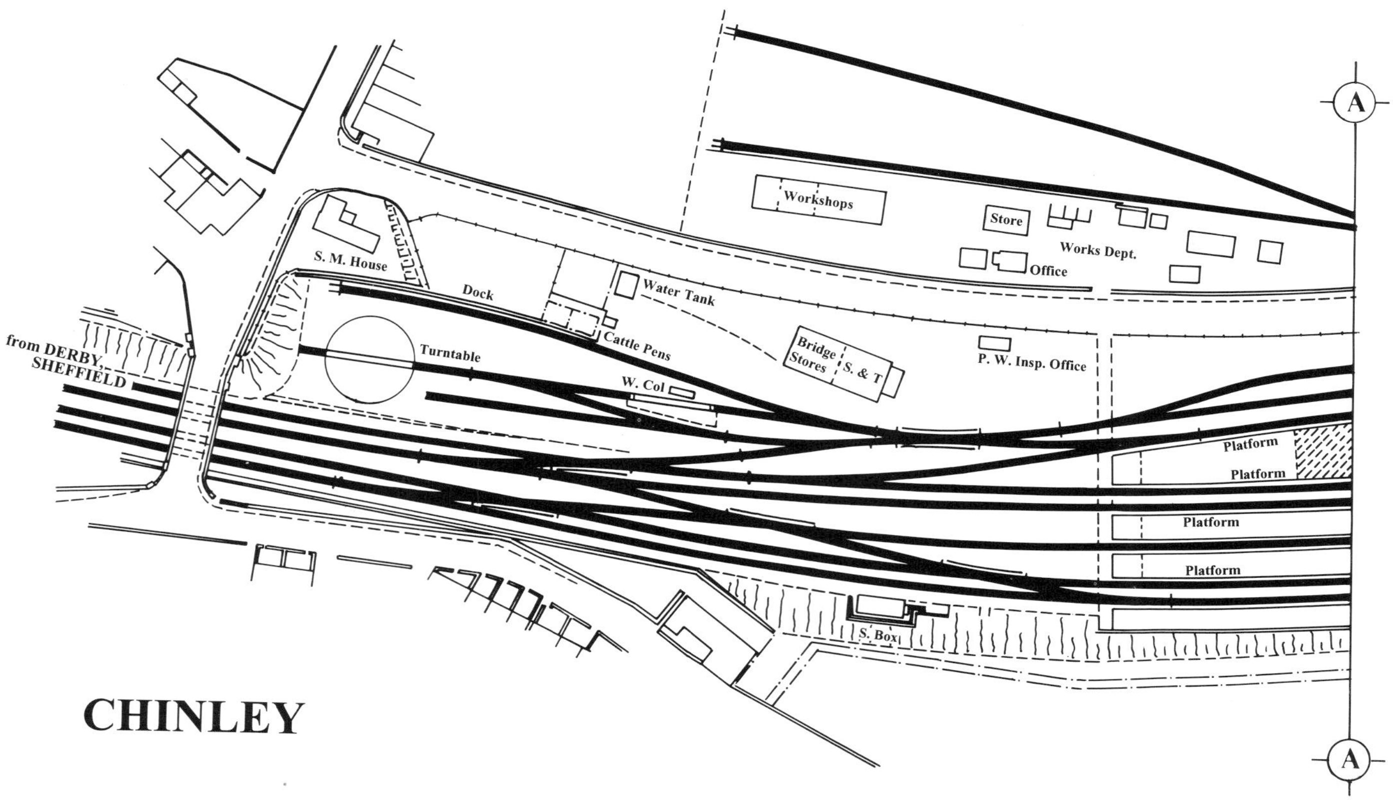

CHINLEY

Chinley Station. A view from the road bridge: reproduced from a contemporary postcard with tones akin to an Impressionist painting, this interesting card shows Chinley station and yard in all its Midland Railway glory. Looking at the neat and tidy layout, the white-painted signals, the arc-roofed coaches and the little engine alongside platform 1, we can only breathe a sigh of nostalgia for such days. The signals are painted, as per Midland fashion with white roundels, not stripes, on their arms - a practice which ceased from around 1912. Interestingly, the postcard was posted from Chinley on Wednesday, April 26th 1905 to Edward Cecil Poultney Esq. in Ulverston. Poultney had received his training on the Furness Railway and was well known as a writer on locomotive and engineering matters. He had been involved with government work in both world wars; awarded the O.B.E., Poultney had been manager of Lentz Patents Ltd. with whom he had been engaged on the development and application of poppet valves for locomotives. *Collection of Brian Hilton.*

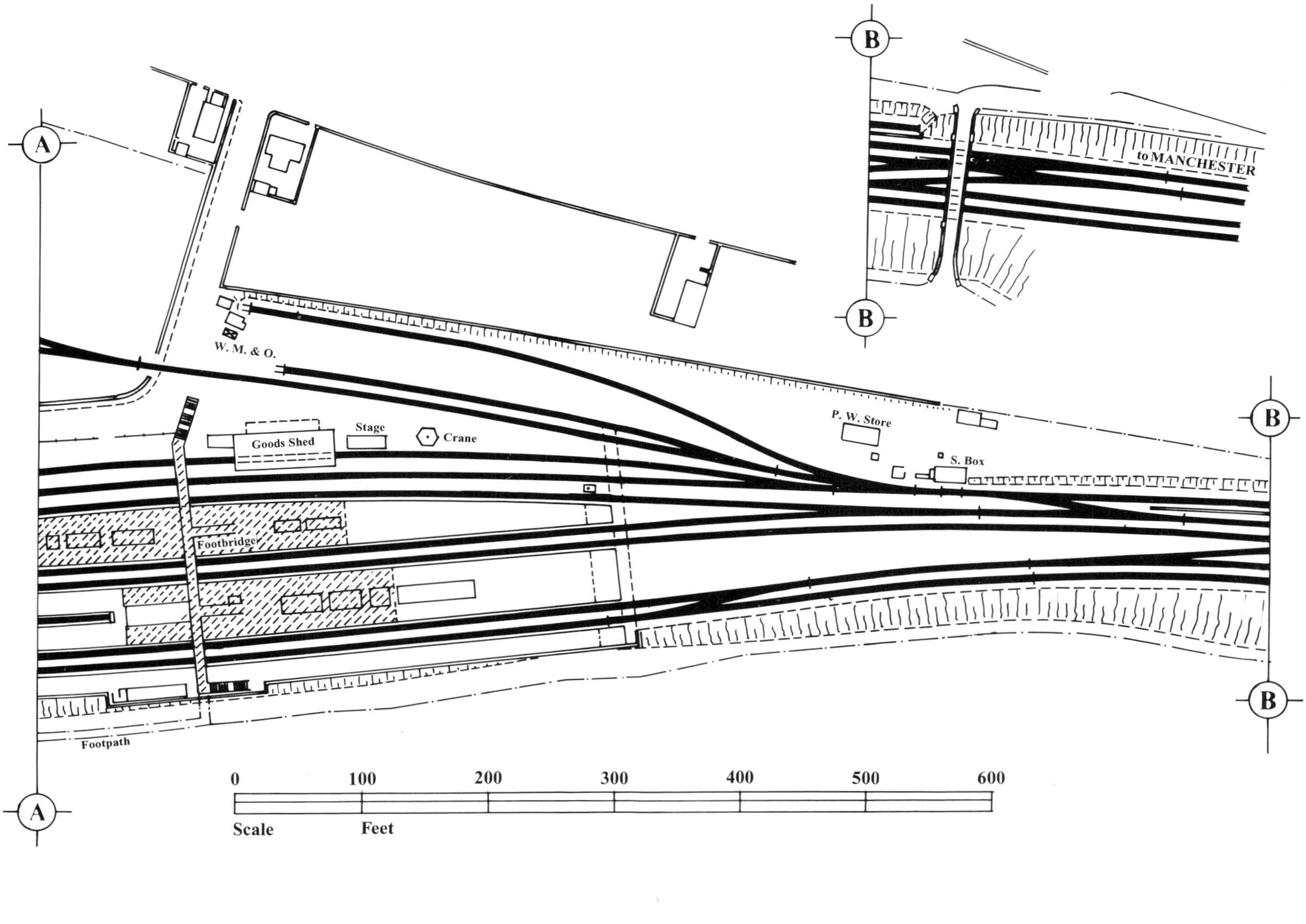

Chinley Station, April 10th. 1953: Looking across the station from platform 5, we gaze across to the bay platform, No.3, from where local trains-to Sheffield, Derby and Buxton departed. Awaiting the "right away" is the 2.30 Chinley to Buxton, a modest one-coach affair, hauled by a Fowler 2-6-4 tank. Time taken for the 12½ mile journey was in the order of 30 minutes. Calling at Chapel-en-le-Frith and Peak Forest, trains left the Midland main line at Buxton Junction to run westwards through Ashwood Dale into Buxton Midland station. Local operating practice decreed that the "right away" had to be given from both sides of the bay before the train could depart. Controlling operations at this end of the station was Chinley Station South Junction box plainly visible at the far end of platform 1. *J.D.Darby*

Chinley Station South Junction, May 17th. 1952: The "Bobby" in the box watches dutifully as "Jubilee" No.**45628** *Somaliland* blows off as it moves away southwards from platform 4 with a Manchester Central to St.Pancras express. *B.K.B.Green*

Chinley Station South Junction, August 30th.1947: Taken from the overbridge that carries Chinley Road over the railway, this fine shot provides a panoramic view over the whole station area. 4F No.**4246**, with tender cab, is heading a heavy Up freight-made up of some forty loaded vehicles-along the Up Slow line. Known locally as "Derby 4s" these workhorses, of Midland parentage, were so common here at one time as to be almost unworthy of note; what memories they evoke now! South Station Junction signalbox can be seen just beyond the stone wall; this was the biggest of the five Chinley boxes, housing 48 levers. Splendidly arrayed is the trackwork, all laid to main line standards. Notice the "scissors" arrangement in front of the bay platform allowing movement from the bay to either the Up Slow (Sheffield) or Up Fast (Derby) lines or from the Fast to Slow lines themselves. An unidentified locomotive stands on the turntable positioned chimney first. *J.D.Darby*

Chinley, Station South Junction, n.d: A spectacular view looking across the junction from the Chinley Road overbridge. 8F No.**48775** vigourously attacks the Up Slow (Sheffield) line with a lengthy through fast freight. I think this picture, more than any other, gives a good idea of the sheer size and breadth of Chinley-more than just a station, a true railway centre.
Martin Welch

Chinley Station South Junction, May 17th.1952: The retaining wall alongside the Up Slow line was known as "The Wall Side." Special instructions were in force at Chinley which permitted the shunting of loaded passenger trains between platforms 1 and 2. This was a practice by no means permitted everywhere; on contacting the signalman at South Station Junction for this manoueuvre, the Station Inspector would request: "Wall Side, Bobby!" Passing alongside this landmark is LMS Compound No.**40910** with a stopping train to Sheffield. *B.K.B.Green*

Chinley Station South Junction, Friday, August 27th.1965: Framed by the Chinley Road overbridge an unidentified 8F approaches the station precincts along the Down Slow (Sheffield) line. Foxline author Mike Bentley, the loco's fireman, keeps a cautious eye on the photographer. *David Birch*

South of Chinley Station, n.d: Chinley Road overbridge is left behind as "Jubilee" No.**45649** *Hawkins* strides out southwards with an express for St.Pancras. The four-track formation continued as far as Chinley North Junction. Notice the Slow (Sheffield) lines on the far side still laid in bull-head rail; nearer the camera, the Fast (Derby) lines, carrying the heavier, faster traffic have been up-graded to flat-bottom status. *A.H.Bryant*

South of Chinley Station, n.d: A leaking top-feed is causing 8F No.**48135** a spot of bother as it blasts its way up the 1-in-90 towards Chinley North Junction with a train of Hopper empties. *A.H.Bryant*

South of Chinley Station, n.d: Clearing Dakin's Bridge (No. 107 in the Ambergate District Bridge Register) and having a tough time by the looks of it, is Stanier 2-6-4 tank No. **42373** at the head of a stopping train to Sheffield. *A.H.Bryant*

Approach to Chinley North Junction, June 4th.1950: Guarding the approaches to Chinley North Junction from the Manchester direction were these two sets of signals. In the background is bridge No.108 known locally as Deansgate Bridge, eight chains beyond is bridge No.109 which rejoiced in the name of Dakin's bridge. These are fine examples of former Midland semaphores, though, as at New Mills, the LMS practice of using flat-capped finials (*a la* LNWR) on top of the posts can be seen. Another example, complete with white-painted spectacle casings is set off to the right, a pure Midland specimen by way of a contrast. The signals, all worked from Chinley North Junction box, were (left to right): Up Slow Distant (Sheffield line), Up Slow Distant (Sheffield line to Derby line), Up Fast Distant (Derby line to Sheffield line), Up Fast Distant (Derby line). All had been replaced by colour lights by the middle of 1952. *J.D.Darby*

Approaches to Chinley North Junction, June 28th.1952: Mention has been made elsewhere of Diesel power on this railway and I offer here a fascinating contrast to our previous shots depicting modern locomotives. Running along the Up Fast (Derby) line is No. **10800** with the 8-coach 11.35 Manchester Central to Derby conveying through carriages for Nottingham. Looking like something of a cross between a Class 20 and an 08 Shunting engine is the largely experimental Diesel-Electric No.10800. Conceived as far back as 1946, the engine was developed as a short to medium-haul locomotive. When this picture was taken, 10800 was undergoing trials prior to spending a short period on the Southern Region. Built initially by the North British company in 1948/50, it was rebuilt by Brush in Loughborough in 1962 in connection with experiments with brushless traction motors. Named, unofficially, "Falcon", 10800 was cut up in 1976. *B.K.B.Green*

Approaches to Chinley North Junction, 1890s: Almost exactly one mile of wild, inhospitable terrain separates Chinley Station from the first of the three junctions on its south-eastern flank. Although numerous new housing developments have sprung up in the area surrounding the village in recent years, the Derbyshire landscape here has retained its isolated, yet starkly beautiful, character despite the intrusion of the railway. Only the fencing has changed in the intervening years as two of Mr.Johnson's beautiful small-boilered 4-4-0s, a "60" Class piloting a "1327" Class, head south through the Peak with an Up express. What might be termed the "classic" Midland express has often been portrayed by a view showing an immaculately-groomed line of clerestory stock of the Bain or Clayton variety. In total contrast, we see a 9-coach express comprising what can only be called a "rag-bag" of stock. Clerestory, arc-roofed, six and even four-wheeled carriages and vans make up this motley-looking assortment. But never mind; what character, what individuality!
Collection of J.Braithwaite

Approaches to Chinley North Junction, n.d: A more uniform style of coaching stock is exhibited by this later picture. Taking the Sheffield (Slow) line is No.**436**, a Deeley rebuild of one of Johnson's "2203" Class of 1893, in charge of 6-coach express. It is worth re-iterating that the Midland had used the Dore and Chinley line for non-stop running from both Cheadle Heath and Chinley to St.Pancras; 186.1 and 175.1 miles respectively. *Author's collection*

Approaches to Chinley North Junction, May 29th.1939: Ancient and modern Midland coaching stock are combined in this stopping passenger train signalled at North Junction for the Derby line. Buxton shed's Fowler 2-6-4 tank No.**2382** steams vigorously along with its five carriages; what price a trip today in a Clayton square-light Clerestory?!
N.Fields

Approaches to Chinley North Junction, June 16th.1951: Showing at a glance the wild, open nature of the landscape here, we look towards Chinley Station as 8F No.**48682** moves effortlessly along the Up Fast (Derby) line with a light load of a mere seven wagons. The white appearance of the leading two wagons is accounted for by their probable use in carrying lime from one of the concerns in the Buxton area. *B.K.B.Green*

Approach to Chinley North Junction, September 4th.1949: Another fine set of semaphores, again using Midland-pattern arms with the LMS-style white spectacle casings and flat-capped finials. In the background is Chinley North Junction box; from here trains on the Slow (Sheffield line) could cross to the Fast (Derby) line or vice-versa. The Home signals here correspond directly to the Distants in the previous view. Distants (left to right) are: Up Slow-to Chinley East Junction, Up Slow-to Chinley South Junction, Up Fast-to Chinley East Junction, Up Fast-to Chinley South Junction. Upper-quadrant arms eventually ruled the day and, as will be seen, framed many a picture at this quite famous location. *J.D.Darby*

Approaches to Chinley North Junction, April 23rd.1949: All four Distants are "on" as a Hughes/Fowler 0-8-0 heads towards the junction with a trainload of timber pit props. No doubt landed at Liverpool, these essential items will be en route for the Yorkshire pits at a time when the railways, and the country at large, maintained a huge dependency on coal as a power source. *J.D.Darby*

Approaches to Chinley North Junction, n.d: Though trains never raced as such, certainly not officially, one can't help thinking, if only for a minute, that a competitive spirit is in the air, along with an awful lot of coal dust, as these two freight trains, drawn respectively by an LMS and a Midland 4F, slog up the 1-in-90 towards the junction. Over on the Sheffield line, on the far side, the Midland engine is leading by a short head. *T.Lewis*

Chinley North Junction, n.d: This is what brought the photographers here. Ample trains, four tracks, a beautiful landscape and just look at those signals! An unidentified 8F with 16 empty limestone hoppers maintains a cautious passage up towards Chinley South Junction. Over on the Sheffield line, 4F No.**44322** waits at the Home signal with a train of coal empties. *Eric Oldham*

At Chinley North Junction the quadruple track formation, which had been formed at New Mills South Junction ended. Here, the Dore and Chinley line ran off in a north-easterly direction towards Cowburn Tunnel, while the Derby line turned south in the direction of Chapel-en-le-Frith. Chinley North Junction box, housing 44 levers and the second largest of the five Chinley boxes, controlled two sets of crossovers. These enabled trains on either the Sheffield or Derby lines (designated Slow and Fast respectively) to change tracks in either direction of running. The diverging nature of the lines, coupled with a fine landscape background, semaphore signals in prominent view and the close proximity of the A624 Chapel to Glossop road has made Chinley North Junction a firm favourite with photographers over the years.

Chinley North Junction, n.d: A rather odd combination of motive power marks out this scene as strong afternoon sun highlights Stanier Class 3 2-6-2 tank piloting Ivatt Class 2 Mogul No.**46443**. Ample steam appears to be available to power the 9-coach train over the Hope Valley line towards Sheffield. *Eric Oldham*

Chinley North Junction, May 8th.1948: The immediate post-war years were difficult ones for photographers. Shortage of film and paper, with much of what was available being of dubious quality to boot, conspired against the enthusiast who wanted to use a camera. Notwithstanding these difficulties, some excellent results were obtained as this fine shot shows. "Jubilee" No.**5628** *Somaliland* heads the 1.50 p.m. Manchester Central to St.Pancras express, made up to 11 coaches, over the junction and south towards Chapel-en-le-Frith. *J.D.Darby*

Chinley North Junction, n.d: At junction layouts, in semaphore days, it was always possible to tell, more or less, in what direction trains were heading. Underlining this, 8F No.**48642** with a train of wagon empties, is signalled to cross over to the Sheffield line. Chinley East's Distant is "off" giving the driver a clear run from here up the 1-in-90/1-in-100 to the mouth of Cowburn Tunnel. Into the tunnel, at 1-in-150, and the line will have levelled out just before daylight is reached. Then the gradient will be in the train's favour, all along through the splendid Derbyshire countryside before a brief climb again, just before Bamford. To the right of the track, by the locomotive, is the Crown and Mitre public house. This was acquired by the Midland Railway when the line here was widened in the early part of the century. It seems the company were not over-anxious to become heavily involved in licensed house management and a recommendation by the Midland's estate agents in August 1904 that the pub be sold was accepted! *A.H.Bryant*

Chinley North Junction September 3rd.1955: One of the all-time classic pictures taken at this beautiful spot is, surely, this one by the late Tom Lewis. Coming up the line under clear signals is "Jubilee" No.**45649** *Hawkins* in charge of a 10-coach Manchester-St.Pancras express. The sixth vehicle is an ex-LMS 12-wheeled kitchen/dining carriage, a standard feature of the London trains over this route in the 1950s. Even when unobserved, their presence in a train was unmistakable: the rapid "four-in-a-bar" rythm of the wheels on the rail joints giving way to a syncopated rattle as the train roared by. *T.Lewis*

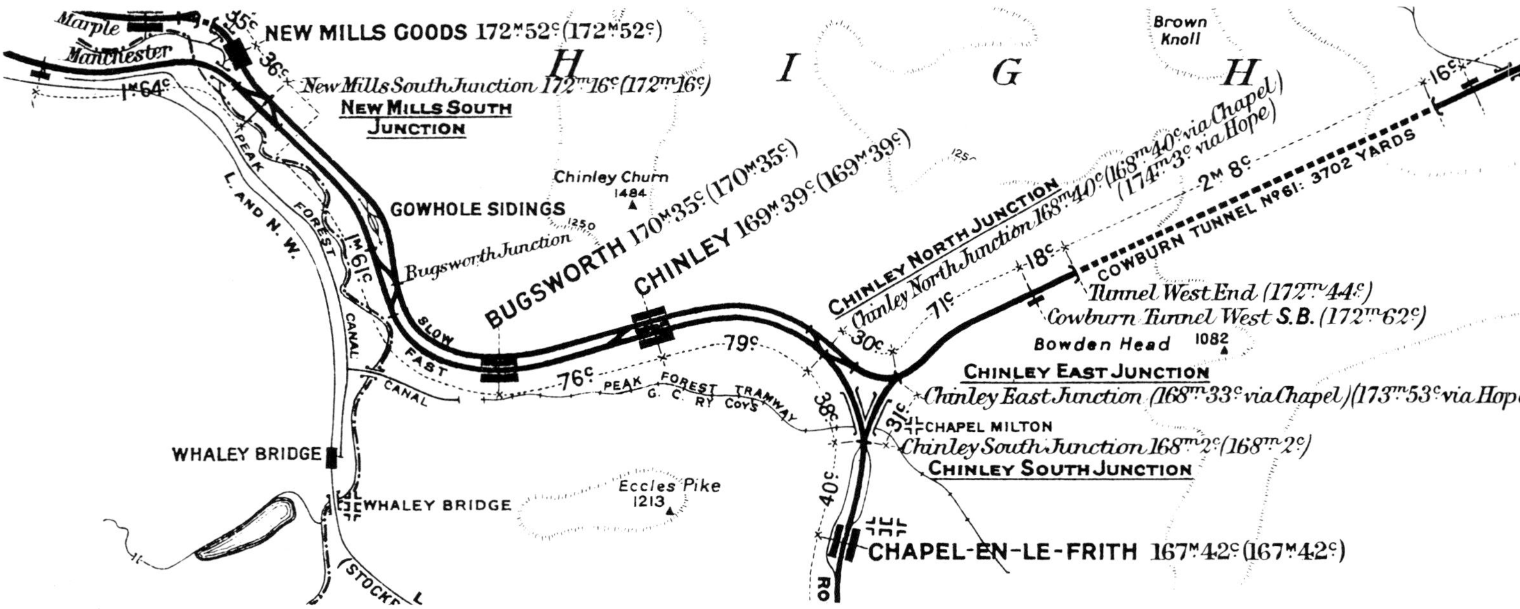

(above). **Chinley North Junction, October 12th.1957**: Showing us what operational possibilities existed at Chinley North: 4F No.**44241** comes over from the Up Slow (Sheffield) line to Up Fast (Derby) line with a lengthy mixed freight train. Chinley South's Distant is "off" so our train will have a clear run at least as far as the Chapel loops. *J.D.Darby*

Chinley North Junction, 1946: 3F No.**3630** has a clear road signalled along the Derby line and as far as Chinley South Junction. The 18-wagon train, plus brake van, is a very typical mixed freight of the immediate post-War period. All credit to photographers who recorded scenes like this at a time of difficult travel and scarce resources. *P.Ward*

Chinley North Junction, 1946: 10 coaches and a van comprisesthe load behind "Crab" No.**2904**. The train is a returning Llandudno to Desford excursion travelling via Sheffield. The train is on the Up Fast line; once out of sight of the camera, the loco will swing over to the left, signalled by the lower of the left hand semaphores, and onto the Up Fast to Up Slow crossover to take the Hope Valley line. By the look on the fireman's face, a good time was had on this North Wales trip, happy days! *P.Ward*

Chinley North Junction, April 22nd.1965: The "Midland Pullman," on its penultimate working south, was mentioned in the Cheadle Heath feature. Here is the two-tone blue and white beauty rounding the curve of the Derby line on its way south. Entering service on July 4th.1960, this 6-coach Diesel-electric all-1st.class train brought a touch of glamour to the former Midland Manchester-London line. Sadly, the "Pullman" only lasted just about six years and its demise heralded the last few years of the line as a through route. The LM authorities placed special store on the prestige train. Stabling and servicing were carried out at the Reddish electric depot-well away from the grime and rigours of steam loco maintenance. Throughout its brief career a rolling stock inspector always travelled with the train; B.T.Barker and D.Morrison were amongst those allocated to this duty. Inspector Barker, in particular, was something of a devotee-even transferring to Hull when workings from there were mooted after the train's withdrawal from the Midland route in 1966.

John Clarke/The Museum of Science and Industry in Manchester

Chinley East Junction was the point where trains on the Hope Valley line could by-pass Chinley station and run south to join the Derby line at Chinley South Junction and vice-versa. In the 1950s and '60s this triangle of lines outside Chinley was a very busy stretch of railway; beyond Chinley South Junction, at Chapel-en-le-Frith, goods loops were provided on both sides of the line. On the Up side of the chord line between Chinley South and Chinley East Junctions, an Outer Home signal was provided for the purpose of drawing trains up clear of Chinley South Junction. The 31-chain chord line ("Chinley South Curve") between these two Chinley junctions was opened on May 19th.1894. It has had something of a chequered history: it was closed to passenger traffic on October 1st.1904, only to re-open on July 1st.1912. The curve was closed again to passenger traffic on January 1st.1917, presumably as a wartime economy measure. Remaining in use, as we shall see, for freight traffic only, until September 21st.1964, the track on the chord line was then taken out of use. As has happened elsewhere, track removal proved hastily conceived and the connection, as a single line, was restored in December 1980.

Chinley East Junction signalbox, with just sixteen levers, was the smallest of the five Chinley boxes. A Midland period II box, it had opened for traffic on October 29th.1893. Its siting must have caused some initial problems for the signalmen, as a Midland record shows it to have been raised as and from April 29th.1894. It was closed when the Chinley South Curve was taken out of use-February 27th.1966. A nice story regarding Chinley East box was passed to me recently. One week before closure, a gang of painters arrived at Chinley station complete with ladders, paint, equipment and instructions to re-paint the box! Questioned by the Station Inspector, the men confirmed their intentions: "yes, the box was definitely to be re-painted!" Apparently, in the hey-day of closures, extra paper savings could be shown if the value of a structure, earmarked for closure or demolition, was increased. Ours is not to reason why.........

Chinley East Junction, April 4th.1960: 8F No.**48663** comes up from Chinley North Junction with a train of empty coal wagons, making a good deal of smoke in the process. Undeterred by the presence of a train, a P.W. gang continue work on the track of the South Curve; no high-visibility vests in those days! *Tom Lewis*

Chinley East Junction, May 9th.1959: An interesting scene giving a good view of the layout here. Coming up the Hope Valley line is B.R. Standard Class 5 No.**73065** with the 4.05 p.m. Manchester Central to Sheffield Midland train. Standing behind the Home signal is 8F No.48694 with an Up Freight. Just behind the brake van is the Chinley South Up Starter (lever number 17) protecting the train in the rear. Under Regulation 4, the 8F and its train would have been required to draw to a stand before the passenger train could have been accepted from Chinley North Junction. *Brian Hilton*

Chinley East Junction, September 6th.1959: A very grimy "Jubilee" No.**45557** *New Brunswick* takes the Hope Valley line and heads towards Cowburn Tunnel with the 9.00 a.m. Manchester to St.Pancras express. Diverted off the normal route via Peak Forest because of weekend engineering work, the train will proceed as far as Doe West junction and round the Totley curve to Dore South Junction thus avoiding Sheffield Midland. On through Bradway Tunnel and then south via Dronfield, Chesterfield and Clay Cross to Ambergate North Junction to regain the former route south to the Capital. *B.K.B.Green*

Chinley North Junction, n.d: An unusual view of the junction, taken from the south side. Waiting at the Home signal on the Derby line is Class **25 070** with a loaded ICI Hopper train from Tunstead Quarry. Next to the signalbox can be seen the sweeping curves of the eastern crossover enabling trains from the Derby line to pass to and from the Dore and Chinley ("Hope Valley") route. Heading towards Sheffield on this line can be seen a 3-car Metro Cammell DMU; heralding the shape of things to come, when such trains form the bulk of the somewhat sparse traffic that passes this spot nowadays. The Midland-pattern manual signalbox here was the second at this location. The box in our picture opened on October 26th.1902, replacing an earlier box that was sited in between the fork of the Sheffield and Derby lines and dated from October 1993. The present signalbox here, named plain "Chinley" is a power box and was commissioned on December 14th.1980. *J.Hooper collection*

Approach to Chinley South Junction, n.d: "All-clear" at Chinley South Junction for an 8F with a train of ICI Hopper empties. The train has crossed the A625 road and is now traversing Chapel Milton viaduct with Chinley South Junction box discernible on the horizon. This viaduct had been built in 1865 and consisted of 15 spans, each 42 feet wide. Once over the viaduct, the loops, referred to elsewhere, were encountered, along with Chapel-en-le-Frith station and Dove Holes Tunnel. Beyond this tranquil setting nowadays, the new A6 trunk road, by-passing Chapel-en-le-Frith and Whaley Bridge, carries its incessant stream of traffic past Chapel Milton Viaduct, Whitehough and the Peak Forest Canal. Would that some more of it could return to the railway! *Norman Jones*

Chinley South Junction, Winter 1967/68: 8F No.**48775** is en route to Buxton with a train of vans as it is caught framed between the fine stone arches on the approach to the junction. In the foreground is the Chinley South Curve leading along from East Junction. The 2-8-0 is on the Derby line from North Junction and is heading towards Chinley South Junction and Chapel Milton Viaduct. *Martin Welch*

Chapel Milton Viaduct. May 17th 1952. Captured in the middle of this fine-looking structure is Class 5 No.**45279** on a gorgeous summer day en route to the Peak and London St.Pancras. The superb Derbyshire landscape is in plentiful profusion; just visible in the left-hand background are the protecting signals for Chinley North Junction. *B.K.B. Green.*

Chinley South Junction takes us to the base, so to speak, of the Chinley triangle-the three junctions on the station's south-eastern flank. Here, the main line to Derby, which had forked south-east at Chinley North was joined by the Chinley South Curve which had split from the Dore and Chinley line at Chinley East Junction. South Junction box, housing 30 levers, had opened for traffic on May 21st.1893, the lever arrangement was altered in the December of that year. Chinley South Junction signalbox closed on May 17th.1970.

Chinley South Junction. June 28th 1952. A view from track-level shows Class 5 No.**45284** passing over the junction with an Up excursion working. *B.K.B. Green.*

Chinley South Junction. September 11th 1948. The omni-present ICI bogie Hoppers are seen to great advantage in this splendid late summer view taken from the road overbridge that spanned the junction layout. 8F No.**8190** (the BR numbering has yet to come into force) is signalled "inside" i.e. into the loop that ran off under the bridge towards Chapel-en-le-Frith. The Chinley South Curve comes in at the bottom right-hand of the picture; each line is provided with identical signals; two Home signals - one each for the main running lines and a lower (Distant) arm to signal entry into the Chapel loops. Notice, again, the provision of splitting Distant arms for both routes - a practice abandoned in later years. Set against a backcloth showing the peak District at its loveliest, this classic view encapsulates to perfection "the railway in the landscape".

J.D. Darby.

Chinley South Junction signalbox. June 1st 1969. Midland boxes underwent a gradual evolution over the years. This structure is to "Period II" style, extant from around the end of the nineteenth century. The frontal glazing is extended to floor-level, while the ends are glazed to waist height only. Midland boxes were painted in "Lemon Chrome" and "Venetian Red", a scheme echoed, albeit feintly, by the maroon and cream of British Railways' days. Notice the primitive WC and the obligatory coal store. Some non-Midland-style repairs have been carried out to the front left-hand window frame!

M.A. King.

Chinley South Junction. June 28th 1952. Crossing to the south side of the junction, we look at 8F No.**48099** working its way along the Up line with a train of coal empties. To the left and right of the through lines can be seen the loops that were set on either side of the track to relieve congestion on this once-busy railway. The loops stretched between here and Chapel-en-le-Frith, the next station along the line. The Up loop, on the far side, 48 chains long, stopped short of the station on the north side. The Down loop, at 37 chains, ran round the Down side of Chapel station and terminated on the south side.

B.K.B.Green.

Approaching Chapel-en-le-Frith, May 21st.1966: BR Standard 2-10-0 No.**92077** approaches the station with an 8-coach RCTS enthusiasts' special, "The East Midlander" from Crewe Works to Nottingham. In the background can be seen the factory of Messrs. Ferodo, manufacturers of friction material for the automotive industry. *Martin Welch*

Chapel-en-le-Frith, same day: The nicely turned-out engine strides towards the station as heads appear out of the windows to greet the advance of a "Peak" (Type 4) Diesel approaching with a Down express. The water tower and station layout, complete with loops on each side, are seen to advantage. *Martin Welch*

Chapel-en-le-Frith Central, 6th.July 1933: Johnson Class 3 4-4-0 No. **777** enters the station with an Up express. Just under the loco is the exit from the Up Goods loop which forked off just beyond Chinley South Junction. *W.Leslie Good*

Chapel-en-le-Frith Central, n.d: a nice view of the station, uncluttered for once by the passage or sight of a train. The cast-iron spandrels supporting the platform awnings are strongly reminiscent of those seen at Withington and Didsbury. Likewise here, the glass in the awnings has been replaced by felted coverings. The station had opened as "Chapel-en-le-Frith" for passengers on Saturday, February 2nd.1867. The "Central" suffix was added by the LMS as and from June 2nd.1924-doubtless to avoid confusion with the neighbouring ex-LNWR emporium. On the Up platform sits the period III Midland Railway signalbox; opened on June 25th. 1905, this replaced two former boxes-one each to the north and south of the station. Notice the structure has a brick base, an unusual feature for a Midland signalbox. LMS-pattern "target" nameboards grace the platforms. These survived until the station closed to passengers on March 3rd.1967.
Douglas Thompson/Robert Humm collection

Chapel-en-le-Frith Central. c.1967. The missing lamps, snow affected platforms and signalman's car parked beneath the canopy. This unidentified Class 8F is all that breathes life into a by now passenger-less station. Perhaps a somewhat melancholy way to end part two but it is hoped the reader has managed to savour the journey - so far!
Martin Welch

Central Station c. 1946: We begin our journey, of necessity, at Manchester Central. Off over the Liverpool line is former Great Central 4-4-0 Class 11B (LNER D9) No.**2303**. Looking spick and span, the handsome engine and its Gresley articulated suburban coaches are framed by the famous 90 ft. high single roof span. Off to the left can be seen the wooden valances of the station's goods shed and behind this the ruined back of the Free Trade Hall. This most famous Manchester building was severely damaged by an incendary attack in 1940; the station, the Luftwaffe's obvious target, received a near miss in the process. Happily, the Free Trade Hall was restored to life in 1951 and the station roof survives to cover the GMEX Centre. *P. Ward*

A Look Back Along the Line

The declared aim of this volume is to cover the New Mills and Heaton Mersey Line from just below Cheadle Heath as far as the base of the Chinley Triangle-the three junctions situated on the south-eastern flank of Chinley station. To refresh readers' palates, and to forge a link with the start of our story, I am offering a selection of pictures as a recapitulation.

The Manchester South District Railway - The Line In Retrospect

With the closure of Manchester Central station on and from May 5th.1969 and the subsequent severance of the line south from Chorlton Junction in mid-August of that year, part of Manchester's railway heritage was lost and a valuable link in the city's public transport system was thrown away.

The 1960s were the age of the car. Those of us now in middle age will remember a time when the private motor vehicle was a rarity; a thing of the commercial traveller, or the rather better-off. Not so in the '60s. Cars like the Mini, the Ford Anglia and the Austin/ Morris 1100 were being produced at prices, and in volumes,that Joe Public could afford. £650 for a brand-new saloon seems incredible by today's standards; in the early part of the decade, that was the going rate.

Blossoming forth too, was the motorway network. At first just the puny M6-the Preston By-Pass, then the M1 and the northern half of the M6; reaching only as far as Cannock Chase at first, it put the north and south halves of the country within reasonable travelling time.

The public, emancipated by their new-found car ownership had several powerful backers. Britain still had a railway system that touched almost all corners of the land. What did they tell us at school-remember? "if you're stranded anywhere in England, you're never more than X miles from a railway station"-and you weren't!

But all this was to change. In 1962, British Railways were running at an annual deficit of over £160 million, after allowing for interest charges. Something, the Government decided, had to be done; the rest is history. The Beeching Report, 1963/64, titled "The Reshaping of British Railways, had far-reaching and irreversible consequences for all rail travellers. So radical was its proposals, so deep-cutting was the Doctor's knife, that, even today, the shock waves can still be felt.

But as the railways' star was settling in the doldrums, that of the motorway constructors and the road transport lobby was in the ascendant. Closure, cut-back and rationalisation were the key words in railway operation in the 1960s. Paradoxically, it was investment in the network that sealed the fate of the South District line and, further south, the Midland route through the Peak. In April 1966, it became possible to travel through from Manchester Piccadilly to Euston by an all-electric service a thing already possible between Manchester and Crewe from as far back as September 1960. Piccadilly became Manchester's prestige station. Airily glamorous, all concrete and glass and, like the new Euston, with a facade and a concourse more akin to an airline terminal than a railway station. If Beeching had had his way, the Dore and Chinley ("Hope Valley") line would have been closed and also, incredibly, the Manchester to Buxton line. But Britain in the 1960s was simply not public transport-minded; the phrase, by and large was not in common use. Road transport was de rigeur and no serious public debate about any imaginative use of the country's rail network was ever entered in to. Beeching and the road transport lobby had won the day: game, set and match.

But what were we thinking of? Indeed, were we thinking at all? It was the late Earl of Stockton (Harold Macmillan) who used the phrase: "selling the family silver" in connection with the first of the Conservative government's Privatisation programmes. But wait; we didn't *sell* this particular "family silver" at all, we gave it away-literally for scrap. SELNEC, "South-East Lancashire and North-East Cheshire", was the first of the regional bodies, formed in 1969, to oversee public transport at what might be loosely termed "County

Throstle Nest East Junction, 1960: The signalbox viewed from the running lines and looking across towards the Bridgewater Canal. The all-timber structure, with hipped gable to the roof, is somewhat reminiscent of the "B" signalbox just outside Manchester Central (see volume I). En route towards the terminus, two 2-6-2 tank engines-Stanier No.**40094** and Fowler No.**40067**-run past coupled together from Trafford Park shed. *W.Wood*

Level." But if SELNEC was anything, it was a bus-minded consortium. It wasn't until 1974 that the Greater Manchester Passenger Transport Authority was formed, and by then it was too late.

Too late to save the stretch of railway we have been studying: Manchester-Stockport Tiviot Dale and Cheadle Heath and Bredbury to Romiley. And too late, it has to be added, to save Manchester Central to Fairfield, Rose Hill-Macclesfield, New Mills-Hayfield, and Bury to Bolton. Muddled thinking, lack of foresight, lack of planning, non-co-operation and lack of central policy-all conspired in a shambles-like mass.

To return to the South District line: what would its future have been, had British Rail not chosen to sacrifice it in 1969? Discounting its use as an inter-city route for a moment, consider the growth of the town of Stockport. Prior to the mid-1960s, Stockport was a market down with a shopping centre that was relatively mediocre. Development of the Merseyway shopping precinct and its eastern extension at Portwood has changed all that. The place is now lively and bustling, the shops are plentiful and people want to go there. Look at the siting of the town's surviving railway station, Edgeley: high up on the A6 and anything but convenient for the town centre and inaccessible from many Manchester suburbs. Now look at Tiviot Dale: only a mere stone's throw from the Merseyway precinct and the true hub of the town and truly accessible from all the eastern suburbs-Bredbury, Romiley, Marple, Woodley and Brinnington. Consider the south Manchester suburbs: as far back as 1910 it was possible to reach Tiviot Dale in only ten minutes from Didsbury; Withington and Chorlton-cum-Hardy just a little longer.

Didsbury, in particular, suffers chronic traffic congestion; lack of off-street parking is a constant grumble and a particular problem. Had the station been retained and the land on which the goods yard stood sensibly used as an adjacent car park, all would have benefited. Proof, if any is needed, is exemplified at places like Hazel Grove where ample car-parking and sensible co-ordination of bus and rail services work for the common good.

Consider, too, the possibilities at Cheadle Heath: a massive land area and a true inter-city site. As a "Parkway" station it would have had few rivals in Manchester. Near to the motorway and surrounded by high-density housing; fast connections to Manchester, Liverpool, Sheffield, Derby, Nottingham, Leicester and London by HST 125 sets-all were there for the taking. Good local connections, too: to south and central Manchester in just minutes. Even allowing for the removal of Central Station, connection with Manchester Piccadilly was perfectly feasible via Cornbrook Junction.

Going a stage further, and setting aside the use of the Midland line as an alternative route to the Capital, what of former services from Manchester and Liverpool to Derby, Leicester, Loughborough, Luton and Nottingham? Given that these are important centres in a major country about to tie stronger links with the European mainland, what price their rail services to and from the Northwest? True, Regional Railways' 158 trains do give connections to most of these places, but nearly all journeys are made via Sheffield and only the odd train uses Totley curve to avoid the city. With hindsight, it does seem extremely foolish and short-sighted that the Midland line was severed between Matlock and Peak Forest.

With the rapid growth of the southern Peak District as a major centre for tourism, the lack of direct rail connections means only one thing: more cars, more congestion and pollution and a reduction in the quality of life for all. Indeed, as I write this piece, the "Derby Now!" magazine reports that the town of Bakewell is suffering from "tourist fatigue" and needs another 2,000 car-parking spaces. In her analysis of the problem, the lady reporter who wrote the article discussed various options to alleviate the throttling of the town, but failed to mention the railway. So inured have we become to living with and being surrounded by traffic, some of us have forgotten or, maybe, just don't know the part once played by the railway in places like Bakewell in the mass-movement of people.

And what of the future? As I complete this manuscript Her Majesty the Queen is about to visit Manchester to officially open Metrolink-our much-vaunted tramway system that connects the former BR Bury and Altrincham lines with the centre of the city. At last, the

Throstle Nest East Junction 1960: The four-track layout from Manchester Central split twice within a short distance from the terminus: firstly at Cornbrook West, where access could be obtained to the M.S.J & A. line via Old Trafford Junction; and secondly, here, at Throstle Nest East where the Derby and Liverpool lines bifurcated. From the signalbox window, we look west towards Trafford Park Junction with the Liverpool line (known here as the "B" lines) sweeping away to the right, alongside the canal. In the centre of the picture, the Derby line, with approaching train, runs in from Throstle Nest South Junction. These far tracks were known as the "A" lines. Off to the left, set up on the banking, are the Cornbrook carriage sidings complete with roofless sheds. The chapel of Henshaw's Blind School can be made out on the far horizon. *W. Wood*

northern and southern suburbs are joined to one another, and a journey to Piccadilly and Victoria stations from the town centre should now be much less of an ordeal.

Metrolink is the most exciting and interesting thing to happen rail-wise in Manchester for many, many years. In its first few months of operation the system appears to bearing fruit, but much more of what Metrolink provides-quality public transport-is needed. Extensions to the system were mooted even before the first rails through the city centre had been laid, and this is where the South District line could play a part once more in Manchester's transport network.

A Parliamentary Bill has already been passed enabling use, once again, of the alignment from Old Trafford to Didsbury. For some years now a programme of bridge re-instatement has been going on all along the line south of Chorlton Junction towards Heaton Mersey. At this moment (summer 1992) one of the last of the 1879 bridges, the old bridge No.16 at the junction of Lapwing Lane and Palatine Road, is being rebuilt. An immensely costly programme, it really is to be hoped that Metrolink get their extension, justifying the large amounts of money spent in protecting the alignment of the erstwhile Midland line, and, moreover, that South Manchester gets some, or at least part, of its railway back.

Beyond Didsbury and up to Heaton Mersey the cutting, alas, is filled in and the alignment has been lost. The accompanying photographs show the burial of Heaton Mersey station and the ruins of the two bridges-the Midland and the CLC pathways over the River Mersey.

We, rightly, criticise and punish, those members of our society who vandalise, burn and pillage our schools, property and telephone boxes. To say: "what would the Victorians think?" is, really, too simplistic; yet we should have stopped before we closed down and demolished railway stations in the heart of suburbs, took away tracks and sold off odd parcels of land for quick bucks. Such things were not provided as a gesture of altruism and it is naive to pretend they were; but we inherited them and we should have used them wisely. The rash and foolish, often random, railway closures of the 1960s and '70s are now being regretted; in some instances reversal, though costly, is possible. Elsewhere, as between Didsbury and Stockport it is not.

Our railway stations deserve better than being turned into hardware shops, pubs and supermarkets, there is abundant land elsewhere for such purposes. Our trackbeds function best as foundations for permanent way, not as "walkways" or "amenity parks." They deserve capital input, investment for the future, not an existence as unofficial rubbish tips and recipients of a Derelict Land Grant. South Manchester could still resound to the sight and sound of a train, sorry, Supertram. Perhaps one day we will be able, once more, to buy a ticket from Manchester to Didsbury.

* * * * * * * *

Workings Around the Throstle Nest Junctions

THROSTLE NEST SOUTH JUNCTION: In earlier times, the Down Home signal for Throstle Nest South had been a disc signal in the Manchester end of Throstle Nest No.1 tunnel. A Starting signal was sited close to Throstle Nest East Junction's Up Home signal (the line to Derby changed direction [Down becoming Up] at Throstle Nest East).

The Home signals were moved to the Chorlton end of the two tunnels and two bridges, and the Starting signal was abolished. This arrangement was the cause of the signalman at TNS being the recipient of certain critical gestures from the train crews!

This was the sequence of operations: The "is line clear?" signal was forwarded to TNS and held there until "train entering section" or, for express trains, "train approaching", was received from Chorlton

Station box. Chorlton Station sent "train approaching" when "train entering section" was received from Chorlton Junction, 902 yards away.

Assuming Throstle Nest East accepted the train and gave line clear on the block instrument, TNE then offered the train to Cornbrook West Junction. Cornbrook West refused, probably a train coming off the MSJ&A or a movement out of Cornbrook Sidings. TNE, therefore, cannot pull off the Home signal.

On the instrument shelf at TNS was an electrical indicator reading "locked" and "free" applying to the lever of the Down Main Home signal. The indicator needle went to "free" under two conditions: a) TNE block instrument at "line clear" and the short approach track to the Home signal showing "occupied". Or: b) TNE block instrument at "line clear" and TNE home signal pulled off.

Given this situation, the train occupies the track circuit, the indicator moves to "free", annunciator gives a short buzz and signalman pulls lever of Home signal. Simultaneously, Cornbrook West accepts the train from TNE, and TNE pulls off the Home and Distant signals. Express driver, having been brought almost to a stand, sees Home and Distant signals come off almost together and assumes that the signalman has either forgotten to forward "is line clear?" or simply forgotten to pull off for him. Displeasure shown when passing the box, either by gesture or shouted comments such as: "first Distant we've missed since leaving Derby!" Rarely a rude whistle-saving steam for the climb up to Central Station perhaps?

In the opposite direction, Throstle Nest South's Up Home signal was also controlled as Throstle Nest East's Starting signal. Levers in both boxes had to be reversed before the signal arm came off; conversely, when either man put their lever back, the arm returned to danger. If the signalman at TNE put back his lever before the engine had passed the Home signal, and the arm went to danger in the driver's face, TNS had to face the music again!

THROSTLE NEST EAST JUNCTION: Until 1957 (or early 1958), the Down Main and Down Slow (Liverpool direction) Home signals at Throstle Nest East were also controlled as the Starting signals for Cornbrook West Junction. A train being refused by TNE could be allowed, after Cornbrook West had sent a special bell signal to TNE, to clear the junction at Cornbrook West. When the dual control was removed, TNE was authorised to accept trains under Regulation 5: "section clear, but station or junction blocked." (Warning arrangement).

Throstle Nest East Junction. Looking towards Central station. 1960: A train from Liverpool hurries past on the "B" lines. By the looks of things, Gresley teak-bodied stock and a Stanier 2-6-4 tank, this is almost certainly one of the Liverpool to Hull/Harwich cross-country trains. These reversed in Manchester Central before departing over the Fallowfield line to Guide Bridge. Here the tank would come off and a 1500V. dc electric loco would haul the train over Woodhead to Sheffield. Cornbrook carriage sidings appear on the right, with Cornbrook West box (featured in volume I) faintly visible in the middle background. The former Cornbrook engine shed, opened in January 1880, was situated down by the canal, directly opposite Cornbrook West Junction. (Q.V.) The site these days can be identified by the bridge where Metrolink passes under the former CLC main line from Liverpool. Down below the railway, the Bridgewater Canal, occupied by a solitary barge, ploughs its murky furrow behind the Pomona Docks and the Manchester Ship Canal. *W. Wood*

Throstle Nest East Junction, signalbox interior, 1960: A rare glimpse of the interior of this large CLC-pattern box. At 6.30 in the morning, signalman David Grindley poses for the camera in front of the 70-lever frame as shafts of early sunlight pour in through the large expanse of window. As mentioned previously, the two sets of lines out of Central were referred to here as "A" and "B". Older signalmen working the box, however, knew them as "Old Route" (A) and "New Route" (B)-the Manchester vernacular of "Rout" invariably being used in lieu of the more normal pronunciation. Confusion could arise at Throstle Nest where the "Up" and "Down" lines-in and out of Manchester Central respectively-became reversed for trains coming going on and off the Derby line. Thus, an express leaving Central on the Down Fast line and bound over the Midland route, crossed onto the Up line once it had passed Throstle Nest East. Down trains coming round from Throstle Nest South on the Derby line became Up trains between here and Central Station! *W. Wood*

Chorlton-cum-Hardy Signalbox, interior 1957: Signalman A.Wright stands in front of the lever frame answering a call from Throstle Nest South on his accepting block, an LNWR-pattern instrument incidentally. Track-circuiting was in place here, witness the indicators on the block shelf with their broad black bars to indicate occupation. Next to these are the brass-cased signal repeaters with their miniature semaphore arms; three lever collars hang beneath the shelf-a reminder of the days before track-circuiting and associated electrical locking of levers. A line diagram is suspended over the block shelf-no sophisticated illuminated affairs just yet! The vee-shaped wooden boards in front of the frame are to assist in pulling over the difficult levers: a case in point being the Up Distant at the far end of the box-1,244 yards from the Home signal.
W.Wood

An Accident at Throstle Nest East

Dawn was just breaking on the morning of December 27th.1950, when a serious accident occurred some 300 yards east of Throstle Nest East junction box. A light engine, J11 No.**64294** en route from Deansgate Goods, had stopped at the TNE Home signal. The crew failed to carry out Rule 55 and the two signalmen at Cornbrook West thought that the engine's description, from Manchester Central, had been cancelled and did not notice the engine pass. (There was no manual block working between the two boxes, and all trains were signalled by describers). When the 7.35 a.m. passenger train to Liverpool was described, all the signals were therefore lowered for it.
The Liverpool train, hauled by 2P 4-4-0 No.**40397**, struck the 0-6-0 head-on (the loco was travelling tender-first). Despite the fact that the goods engine's brakes were hard on, the locomotive was driven forward a distance of approximately 360 yards. There was severe damage to the leading coaches of the passenger train: telescoping occurred between the first two vehicles, a brake third and a third class. Both coaches had timber bodies on steel underframes and ordinary buffers. The two engines and the first two coaches of the Liverpool train came to rest just on the west side of the junction where the Derby line ran off. Sadly, the fireman of the goods engine and one passenger in the Liverpool train died from their injuries. The Inspecting Officer, Colonel Mc.Mullen, recommended that the cancellation of a train description should require the co-operation of both sets of signalmen (hitherto, it had only required an indication from the box in the rear) and that track circuiting and modern block controls be extended forward from Cornbrook to cover the area controlled by Throstle Nest East.

Trafford Park Junction Signalbox, 1964: The impressive frontage of this all-timber structure is seen to good advantage here. There were in fact 61 levers in the frame (an addenda from volume I). The "extra" lever was No. 19A which worked a signal governing movement from the Down Loop to the Down Main. The last turn worked here was on Sunday, August 1st. 1971, after which the new signalling between Cornbrook and Glazebrook (worked from the London Road power box) came into operation. *W. Wood*

Trafford Park Junction 1964: Leaving Throstle Nest East and going west along the Liverpool line, trains encountered Trafford Park Junction. Standing on the bank, the photographer faces Manchester Central. Coming down the line, a Stanier 2-6-4 tank is about to take the road off to Trafford Park shed. On the adjacent line, the Home signal clatters down as an engine comes off shed en route towards the terminus. This part of the junction gave access also to Trafford Park Sidings as well as the lines of the Manchester Ship Canal. In the background, behind the home signals, the line round from Throstle Nest South Junction runs in to join the Liverpool line. The large building on the left-hand side needs no introduction to Mancunians-this is the famous Old Trafford football ground. The station serving the ground, known as United F.C. halt, parallels the track on the far left. *W. Wood*

Seymour Road Signalbox, 1927: This quite unique picture, taken by the late G.H.Platt, was discovered too late to be included in volume 1. One of only two known pictures of the box, it shows one of R.M.Deeley's 0-6-4, "Flatiron" or "Block" tanks passing with an Up South District Local train. The coaching stock is made up of one of David Bain's close-coupled 48 ft. arc-roofed bogie suburban sets introduced for South District services in 1903. Comprising nine vehicles: 2 x brake thirds, 3 x ordinary thirds, and 4 x first class, they were the first examples of bogie coaches used for these services on a regular basis. *G.H.Platt*

Between Seymour Road and Chorlton-cum Hardy c.1929: Taken from the Stamford Road (later Brantingham Road) overbridge, this view looks north as a 5-coach Up express thunders past hauled by LMS Compound No.**933**. Alongside the Up line is evidence of excavation work: some of this is carried over onto the Down line, just by the fogman's hut. Ahead is bridge No.10A (constructed in 1912) which carried gas and water mains belonging to Manchester Corporation. Running alongside Manchester Road, just behind, was another bridge (No.10) which carried water mains, again owned by the city Corporation. The earthworks belong to a culvert (bridge No.11) with a span of 3 feet. Just visible on the left-hand side are building works which evidence suggests are the new Chorlton Baths. Now known as the Chorlton Leisure Centre, the foundation stone of this building was laid in March, 1928. A fair assumption is that the culvert was laid under the line to take the discharge water from the new baths. This caused disruption to the railway and resulted in the re-siting of the Down I.B.Home signal (which replaced Seymour Road) between Chorlton station and Throstle Nest South Junction from ahead of its original position, just behind the fogman's hut, to a point in front of the lattice-girder pipe bridge and seen in the photograph here. *G.H.Platt*

Chorlton-cum-Hardy Station, Signalbox and goods shed looking towards Throstle Nest South Junction, 1957: The signalbox at Chorlton-cum-Hardy was a CLC timber-built structure with a 24-lever frame. Ahead in our view is the splendid double-arm Up Home signal; worked by lever number 23 this was a CLC-pattern semaphore with a wooden post and cast-iron finial. In front of the Brantingham Road overbridge was the Down Starter-lever number 4 with a shunt arm (number 3) beneath. Sited here, also, was Distant arm to control entry into the Intermediate Block section which had replaced the old box at Seymour Road. The nameboard on the front of the box is an LMS appendage which was later replaced by the modern LMR maroon enamelled end boards. *W.Wood*

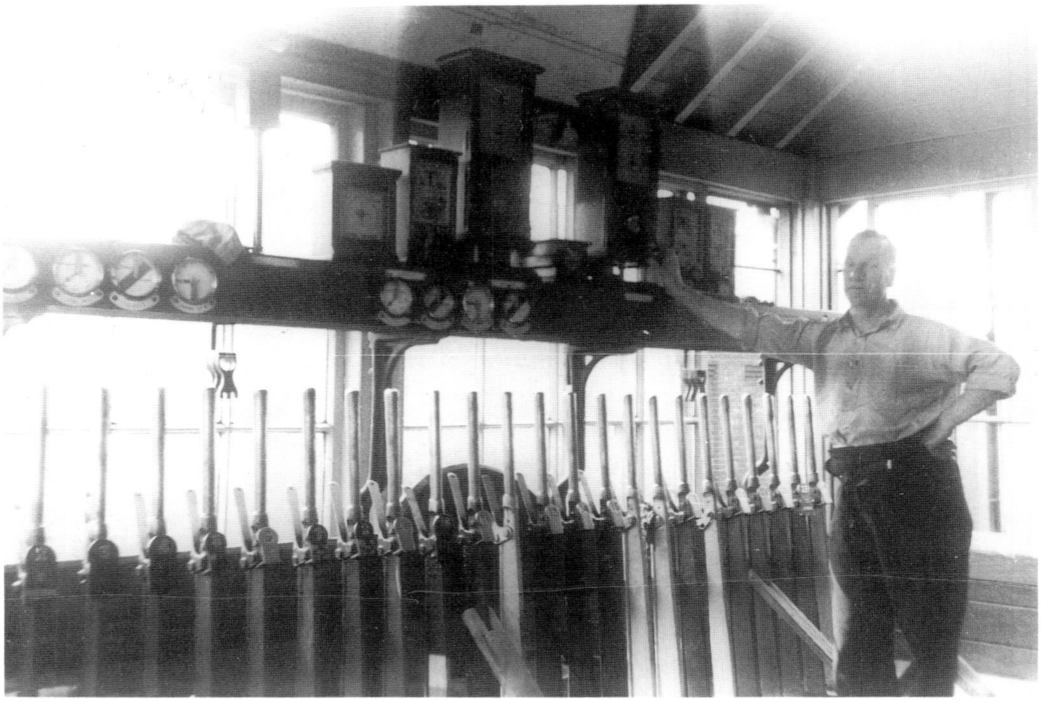

Throstle Nest South Junction, 1957: I had given up hope of ever seeing a really good picture of the box here. Remarks were made in volume I about the difficult location of the structure and I had offered the picture concerned in good faith as being the only likely record of this fascinating place. My beliefs were confounded by Bill Wood, one of the signalmen at T.N.S. in the 1950s, who had the foresight to photograph several locations, this one included, in the Old Trafford area. An essential part of the working the box here was "blocking the curve" to the signalman at Chorlton Junction, i.e. anticipating just how quickly the man at Trafford Park Junction would clear the freight traffic for the sidings there and the Urmston (Liverpool) direction. The last turn worked here was on Friday, March 20th.1970.
W.Wood

South of Chorlton Junction, September 9th.1958: From Mauldeth Road West we look over towards Withington Road with the Broughton Park Rugby ground just behind the railway. Receiving the "right away" is "Britannia" Pacific No.**70042** *Lord Roberts* with the 8-coach 4.25 p.m. express to London St.Pancras. Cutting across the far flank of the rugby ground is the line from Fairfield, then, too, still a busy entity with its own main line expresses and freight traffic. Sadly, today, only nature's wilderness is visible from this point; no more the roar of the trains to distract the Rugby players in their scrums. *W.A.Brown*

Leaving Chorlton Junction, August 21st.1946: "Jubilee" No.**5655** *Keith* was something of a regular sight on expresses to and from St.Pancras over the Midland line. Here, on a Wednesday afternoon, the sun shines, the war is over and all appears clean, neat and tidy as the train heads south. The usual 8-coach formation has been augmented by the addition of an LMS full brake next to the tender. *William Lees*

Hough End Fields, September 24th.1960: Showing the still-open nature of the landscape in this part of South Manchester is this view of Royal Scot No.**46162** *Queen's Westminster Rifleman* nearing the end of its journey with the 10.25 a.m. express from St.Pancras. The Nissen-style buildings along the lineside were part of an anti-aircraft battery installed here during the Second War. *W.A.Brown*

Between Didsbury and Heaton Mersey, May 3rd.1952: The regular favourites of "spotters" in the 1950s, myself included, were the "Jubilees". Here, No.**45629** *Straits Settlements*, barks her way up the rising gradient towards Heaton Mersey and Cheadle Heath with a 9-coach express bound for St.Pancras. In the distance is Kingsway (A34) and behind that the Styal line. The allotments on the left of the picture still exist; the swathe of ground alongside the Down line now harbours a wilderness of bushes, small trees and blackberry thorns, all but obliterating what is now the "walkway" from this point. *B.K.B.Green*

Kingsway overbridge, between Didsbury and Heaton Mersey, 1920s: I mentioned in volume I the regular incidence of the Deeley Midland 0-6-4 or "Block Tanks" that worked South District Line local trains. Here is one such engine working bunker-first and making energetic progress with a close-coupled Bain arc-roofed set of non-corridor stock. A period touch is provided by the gentleman in the Homburg hat sat straddled aside the fence. The elaborate bridge with its arched section over the footpath still stands; sadly, the adjacent land and trackbed is nowadays unrecognisable under the jungle that thrives here since the line's closure in 1969. *Author's Collection*

Heaton Mersey Station, June 23rd.1948: We saw "West Country" Pacific No.**34005** *Barnstaple* at work on the South District in volume I. The sight of this picture of the same engine at Heaton Mersey later in the June of 1948 was irresistible. Again, performing in the interchange trials of the early post-Nationalisation period, *Barnstaple* is seen storming along towards the Mersey Viaduct at the head of the 1.50 afternoon express to St.Pancras. *R.E.Gee*

The remains of Didsbury Station, May 19th. 1974: A rather ghostly scene is set as we look towards West Didsbury from the Up side of the line to view the remains of the platform buildings. Twelve years on from this picture, nature has almost re-gained a total stranglehold here and it is now difficult to imagine the existence of a railway line at all. Within the last two years, an outline plan has been hatched to cover the alignment and build a shopping precinct over the top. At the same time, sufficient room would be left beneath to provide for a station and railway based on a Metrolink extension running from Old Trafford to East Didsbury. *Raymond Keeley*

Heaton Mersey, October 26th. 1969: Looking towards Didsbury, this was the depressing view as the contractors lifted the track. They made short work of the task; all was gone by the end of November. *A.C.Gilbert*

(above), **Cheadle Heath North Junction. 15th September 1979.** The years since passenger services were withdrawn have not been kind to Cheadle Heath. Its junction status is now nothing more than a single lead to enable the two lines from the south to merge into one, a situation determined by construction of a concrete bridge that will carry the railway over the planned M63 motorway through Stockport. The weed-strewn formation to the right indicates the route of the erstwhile main line, now severed at a point where the high level bridge passed over the Cheadle to Stockport Tiviot Dale line. *M. Thorley*

(top right). **Gotterdammerung**: the end of Cheadle Junction box, as it disappears in a pall of smoke and flames, the result of an arson attack on the evening of April 20th. 1985. *Author's collection*

(centre-right). **"Three vast and trunkless legs of stone...."**: the remains of the high-level bridge (The Mersey Viaduct) as seen in June, 1974. In the background, the CLC line from Godley to Glazebrook East Junction is still in operation. *Raymond Keeley*

(lower-right). **Georges Road Yard/ Wellington Road Tunnel, March 16th.1983**: the yard trackwork has been lifted, the semaphore arms have gone, and the signalbox is a windowless hulk. Below, on the former Up line, headed by Class 40 **40085**, a track-lifting crane removes a panel of concrete-sleepered track, salvaged, no doubt, for use elsewhere.

Winter Daydreams: An evocative scene by Raymond Keeley at Heaton Mersey in the winter of 1969, shortly after the track had been lifted from Chorlton Junction to Cheadle Heath North Junction. We are looking at the buildings on the Up side, notice the similarity between these and the station at Chorlton-cum-Hardy. A gradient post lingers as a reminder of the uphill struggle faced through here by engine crews as their charges laboured southwards. *Raymond Keeley*

Heaton Mersey Station, April, 1974: Reflecting on the demise of the South District line, Raymond Keeley mentioned that, maybe Heaton Mersey Station would be the subject of some archaeological dig in a thousand years time. Should that happen, the diggers will certainly have some food for thought about our transport policies. In the background, a bulldozer is busily pushing earth forward to complete the entombment of the cutting. The station buildings cost just £168 to demolish. *Raymond Keeley*

Chinley Station. April 18th 1981. Steam is long gone, and the "Hoppers" are now Diesel-powered. Class 25/2 Sulzer 1250 H.P. Diesel-Electric No.**25086** roars through the station with 14 loaded Limestone Hoppers, en route for ICI Winnington, Northwich. Further dilapidation has taken place since the previous picture was taken: the station footbridge is now roofless, the canopies on platforms 2 and 3 have been removed, the tall yard lamps have gone and, over to the right, platforms 5 and 6 are slowly being engulfed by the ravages of nature. One can only say that the idyllic-like surroundings offer something of an antidote to the depressing scene that this picture paints. *J. Davenport.*

Chinley Today

A passenger turning up at Chinley in 1992 who, maybe, knew the station perhaps 25 or 30 years ago could be forgiven for thinking that he, or she, had come to the wrong place. "A pale shadow of its former self" has become almost a cliche, so often has it been used to describe places in railway lore that have succumbed over the years to the endless onslaught of rationalisation. I stood on the sole remaining platform with a friend of mine in September 1990. Martin had frequented the place in his scouting and hiking forays in the 1950s and '60s. He shook his head; "this can't be the same place, I used to go in the waiting room just there and warm myself by the fire. Where has it all gone?" But gone it has. Gone too, the trains, the buildings, the goods yard, the turntable, the signalboxes and the men. Jack Baines, Bill Beswick, Norman Birkett, Jack Harding, Joe Cox and Paddy Green. No more the soup pot on the stove in the mess room on number 5 platform with its locally-shot rabbits, potatoes and bacon ribs-always on the go to provide tasty morsels for the "lads." No more the sheep and ducks which might appear on number 1 platform, straying and waddling onto the tracks and chased by staff frantically trying to warn off the errant animals before the "Hoppers" cut short their necks. Chinley in the summer of 1992 is served by just 11 Up and 9 Down regular weekday trains en route to and from Sheffield. These use the later route from Romiley and travel via Reddish North and Belle Vue into Manchester Piccadilly. The 158s rush through en route to and from Manchester and East Anglia; still it is possible to photograph the "Hoppers" at Chinley North Junction.

Thus came the wheel of railway history full circle at Chinley.